Cultivating Common Ground

Marlene —
Best wishes (keep Cultivating
common on Ground)

Dan Hanson

Cultivating Common Ground

Releasing the Power of Relationships at Work

Daniel S. Hanson

Butterworth-Heinemann

Boston   Oxford   Johannesburg   Melbourne   New Delhi   Singapore

Library of Congress Cataloging-in-Publication Data
Hanson, Daniel S., 1945–
    Cultivating common ground : releasing the power of relationships
at work / Daniel S. Hanson.
        p.   cm.
    Includes bibliographical references and index.
    ISBN 0-7506-9832-2 (alk. paper)
    1. Job satisfaction.   2. Interpersonal relations   3. Organizational
behavior.   4. Work environment.   I. Title
HF5549.5.J63H278   1997
650. 1'3—dc21   97-7402
                                                                            CIP

British Library Cataloguing-in-Publication Data
A catalogue record for this book is available from the British Library.

The publisher offers special discounts on bulk orders of this book.
For information, please contact:

Manager of Special Sales
Butterworth–Heinemann
225 Wildwood Ave.
Woburn, MA 01801-2041
Tel: 617-928-2500
Fax: 617-928-2620

For information on all business publications available, contact our
World Wide Web home page at: http://www.bh.com

10 9 8 7 6 5 4 3 2 1

Printed in the United States of America

A Life without people, without the same people day after day, people who belong to us, people who will be there for us, people who need us and whom we need in return, may be rich in other things, but in human terms, it is no life at all.

. . . RABBI KUSHNER

Contents

Acknowledgments   ix

Prologue: The People Who Grew Vegetables   xi

Part I   Driving Relationships Underground   I
- **I**   Our Struggle with Relationships at Work   3
- **2**   Digging Deeper: How We Got Disconnected   15
- **3**   The Hawthorne Revelation   23
- **4**   The New Organization: A Renewal of Relationships or the Final Blow?   33

Part II   Bringing Relationships into the Open   53
- **5**   Four Reasons to Care   55
- **6**   Embracing Our Fear of Each Other   67
- **7**   From *I* to *We* without Losing *Me*   85

Part III   Cultivating Common Ground: A Process for Building Community at Work   97
- **8**   What's in a Metaphor?   99
- **9**   Clearing Out Old Assumptions   103
- **10**   From Swords to Plowshares   115
- **11**   Discovering Common Ground   121
- **12**   Fertilized with Meaning   129
- **13**   Sowing Seeds and Nurturing Relationships   135
- **14**   Working the Soil Together   143
- **15**   Growing through Conflict   147
- **16**   Living in Harmony   163
- **17**   Celebrating the Harvest   167

Part IV   Relationships and the New Organization   171

   18   The People Discover New Gardens   173

   19   The Changing Workplace   177

   20   A Need for Leadership and Leaders   181

   21   The Future Is Ours if We Learn to
           Care for Each Other   187

Epilogue: A Weekend with Grandpa   193

References   199

Index   203

Acknowledgments

I wrote this book in the middle of my own struggle with relationships at work. At the core of my struggle was my relationship with the organization itself. After a midlife bout with cancer, I had become increasingly aware of the shadows cast by a dysfunctional system that sought to guarantee its own survival at the expense of people and relationships. I had grown frustrated with quick-fix programs designed to make the organization healthy again. What I saw when I took a long, hard look inside the organization was a reinforcement of the win-lose competitive paradigm and a rebirth of rugged individualism reinforced by antientitlement messages from consultants and gurus who encouraged us to develop good habits, take charge of our own careers, and create "Me, Inc." Frankly, I'd had enough. I was ready to leave the organization to teach, write, and consult.

I am still struggling. However, after talking and listening to others inside the organization I know that I am not alone in my struggle. While doing research for this book, I encountered people from all types of organizations, including health care, business, government, and not for profit, who were struggling to hold themselves and their relationships together in the midst of change. I was humbled and inspired by what I saw. By their example, they revealed to me the true meaning of community at work.

I have decided to stay inside the organization—at least for now, because I believe the organization needs people who care. The spirit of caring is beginning to come to the surface again. We must keep it alive and growing. In truth, the spirit is alive only because some people never let it die in the first place. Thus my first acknowledgment goes to the people inside the organization who never stopped caring for their work and each other, whose stories are seldom told because they are too busy holding a life and task in common.

My second acknowledgment goes to my partner in life, whose love and care made it possible for me to find connections in a disconnected world and to stay at least partially intact in the middle of it all. To Sue, whose love and support hold me always.

I must also acknowledge James Frank Mossman, who gave me a living definition of what it really means to hold a community together. Your insights, James, helped shape my thinking about relationships at work and enriched the content of this book. Thank you, especially, for the story about the harvest and for giving me permission to use it. Most of all, thank you for being there for me when I needed someone to care.

My acknowledgments would not be complete if I failed to mention my friends at Butterworth–Heinemann who helped bring this book to print. A special thanks to Karen Speerstra, who encouraged me to keep writing, granted me a little extra time to complete my manuscript, and counseled me along the way.

Prologue
The People Who Grew Vegetables

There once was a group of people who grew vegetables in a kingdom that was known for its fine agricultural products. The kingdom was very large. Thousands of people worked there. Indeed, the kingdom was so large that it was often referred to as the Great Kingdom, a title that pleased the king, because he was convinced that bigger must be better.

There was something about the people who grew vegetables that set them apart from the other groups who worked in the Great Kingdom. To be sure, they grew vegetables of the highest quality. But so did the others. What set them apart had more to do with the way they went about their work. Like the others, they cultivated the ground together, planted seeds, nurtured their growth, and harvested when it was time. But unlike the others they did it with love and care for each other as well as their work. What's more, they were convinced that caring for each other actually contributed to the joy of their work and the quality of their vegetables.

The people who grew vegetables did more than talk about caring. They showed it by their behavior. They made certain that everyone in the group found a challenging and meaningful role. And no matter how busy they were, they always had time to be present for each other when someone needed a helping hand or a shoulder to cry on.

The other people who worked in the Great Kingdom were never quite sure about the people who grew vegetables. Indeed, more often than not, the people who grew vegetables drew suspicious glances. "They seem to be having way too much fun," the others would criticize. But no one could criticize the quality or the output of their work. Thus for the most part, everyone, including the king and his advisors, left them alone.

Every now and then a new head gardener would come along and attempt to persuade the people who grew vegetables to be more businesslike in their dealings with each other and those outside their division. But these head gardeners never got very far. The people continued to care for each other and their work just as they always had. Not because they thought they were better than the others. They just did not see any reason to change. Occasionally one of them would leave to join another division or to work for a more progressive kingdom, but more likely than not that person would return with stories about politics and people who seemed to care only for themselves. The people who grew vegetables were perplexed by this. "How could anyone find joy in putting others down?" they would ask each other.

One day, a stranger came to visit the king. He came to deliver an important message. He warned the king that other kingdoms were reengineering their work processes and cutting costs in their systems. He admonished the king that he too must reengineer before it was too late. The stranger was known as the Knight of Reengineering.

The people had heard about the Knight of Reengineering from their friends in neighboring kingdoms. Rumors began to spread about layoffs and heavier demands on work schedules. But the king called a special meeting and reassured all the people, including the people who grew vegetables, that the Knight of Reengineering brought only good news. He talked about the need for change and the importance of quality and teamwork. The king announced that the Great Kingdom was experiencing competitive pressure from other kingdoms and that it had to improve its work processes. The king said that people were the backbone of the Great Kingdom and that he was relying on everyone to cooperate and become involved. He talked of teamwork and commitment.

The people who grew vegetables wondered what the king meant by this new jargon. They had been involved and committed for a long time. They also wondered what teamwork was all about and whether it was anything like what they had experienced over the years cultivating the ground together while caring for each other. They were anxious to learn more. At the same time, they were cautious.

Soon after the king announced the new program, a seminar was scheduled, and all the people were required to attend. While attending the seminar, everyone learned about working in teams. Like the others who attended, the people who grew vegetables listened to the messages with great interest. After two whole days of "teaming," everyone returned to work equipped with all the latest understanding about teamwork and an armful of the latest tools for teams.

The day after the seminar, the people were instructed to form process improvement teams. At first, the experience of working in new teams was exciting and everyone learned many new skills, including the people who grew vegetables. They also discovered that some of what they had been doing was not necessary, and they learned new, more efficient ways. "This is good," the people said, "If only we had known this sooner we could have grown even better vegetables."

One day, something happened that shocked and saddened the people who grew vegetables. An announcement was sent to all the people of the Great Kingdom that Ralph was retiring. Ralph was a kind and gentle man who had grown vegetables for forty years. The people who grew vegetables could not help but wonder at the news.

As recently as last month Ralph had talked about the importance in his life of the people with whom he worked and how he intended to work at least another five years before retiring. After talking with Ralph the people stopped wondering. They discovered that the decision to leave had not been Ralph's. The king and his advisors had decided that Ralph was no longer needed. The people who grew vegetables were saddened by the loss of Ralph. They recalled what a wise mentor he had been for the younger members of the group and the times that he had been there for them and they for him.

The people who grew vegetables were soon to discover that Ralph was not the only victim of the Knight of Reengineering. Soon after Ralph left, Janet was laid off. The people remembered how Janet had been a source of harmony for the group, always seeking to find common ground when conflict surfaced. They remembered the famous feud between the growers and the harvesters and recalled how, through the efforts of Janet, the group had painfully confronted the issue. The conflict had left some wounds that healed slowly at first. Later, however, the incident became a source of bonding and a lesson that encouraged the people to design a process whereby they could learn from conflict by dealing with it openly in the spirit of dialogue. Indeed, the people discovered that conflict can be a source of growth for the individual as well as the group.

The people who grew vegetables were angered by what they saw happening to their friends. But the king reassured them and presented a severance package to those who were leaving. Not a package fit for the king himself, but a fair shake nonetheless.

"Perhaps the king is right," the people said to one another, "After all, he is trying to be fair." But in their hearts they knew better.

The layoffs continued. Before the purge was over, ten of the fifty-four people who grew vegetables no longer worked in the Great Kingdom. Those who were left were saddened by the departure of their friends, but with the new, heavier work load they had little time to reflect on the past. They were under pressure to perform and frightened by the threat of losing their own jobs. However, on the rare occasions when there was time to look back, the people would long for a time when they could care again.

After a few months had passed, the Knight of Reengineering left the Great Kingdom to warn other kingdoms that they too must prepare for a new, more competitive era. For a period of time thereafter the Great Kingdom flourished and profits improved. But the people who grew vegetables were never the same. Some of them left on their own accord in the hope of finding a place where they could care again. Those who remained continued to attend team seminars and learn about working together from consultants who had never experienced the joy of cultivating common ground together while caring for each other. Without that experience, how would they ever know the true value of people like Ralph and Janet, who served roles far more important to the well-being of the group than merely doing their jobs?

Now and then the people who grew vegetables gather outside the Great Kingdom to reminisce. They reflect on what it was like to cultivate common ground with a group of people who loved each other and their work and how it brought joy to their lives. They wonder whether they will ever experience the joy of caring again.

Driving Relationships Underground

Do not cut yourself off from community, but work and
be active in the community, with love for your fellow human
beings, for what are you all on your own?

...HILLEL

If a way to better there be, it lies in taking a full look
at the worst.

...THOMAS HARDY

I

Our Struggle with Relationships at Work

It later became clear to me that no matter what we do in science or any other area, it will not help if we don't find a way to be related to each other at a deep level.

... DAVID BOHM

If you work in an organization, I don't need to tell you that the story about the people who grew vegetables is make believe. After all, it is naive to think that people could love and care for each other the way the people who grew vegetables did and still do what is needed to keep the Great Kingdom profitable and growing. Even if it were a true story, the facts of life in the modern organization would be enough to kill the myth.

Life is not as simple as it appears in make believe. In real life the organizational demands for growth and profits override the time and effort it takes to build caring relationships. What's more, to care is to risk going against the flow of a system that rewards loyalty, individual effort, superior political skills, rational behavior, and hard work. To paraphrase the words of a successful executive who agreed to critique one of the early versions of this book, "Caring too much can be hazardous to one's career."

To make matters worse, even when we do take time to care for each other at work our efforts are frequently met with a lackadaisical, care less attitude from those who stand to benefit the most. People bring all kinds of personal baggage with them to work. That's why managers who have lived inside the organization for any reasonable length of time say that the idea that we can live as one big happy family is an illusion. They say, the best way to get along at work is to leave caring for each other at home or in the church where it belongs. In other words, stick to business.

Caring relationships at work are troublesome in a rational world. Along with caring relationships come claims and responsibilities. And if that isn't enough to scare us away, add the fact that caring relationships are unpredictable, chaotic, and yes, emotional. We never know what might happen if we care for someone. We might get into all kinds of emotional stuff. As a result, we might find it hard to make tough decisions for the sake of the organization, such as laying off excess people or firing a bad employee. Relationships at work are further complicated by the current issues of diversity and harassment. Many managers are afraid to get close to people for fear they will say the wrong thing or make the wrong gesture. Indeed, caring relationships at work are troublesome. We would rather not deal with them.

For all the foregoing reasons and more, we have for many years pretended that caring relationships between people at work are bad for business. We convinced ourselves that we were better off and would make more rational decisions if we maintained a distance from each other. So we buried our relationships, kept them hidden behind a facade of rational thinking, and became artists at protecting ourselves from each other. On occasion it would appear that we cared. But for the most part our caring was pseudocaring, the kind that doesn't go below the surface gestures of a friendly "hello" or "How are you?" that we don't expect to be answered. When someone truly needed a helping hand, we hid behind the invisible shield called "the organization." After all, we were told, the organization must be profitable and grow. Because what is good for the organization is good for progress, and progress is good for people. After a while, we got so good at denying our relationships that we forgot how to care. Worse yet, we grew to be afraid of each other.

Where Did Caring Relationships Go?

Denying caring relationships at work does not make them go away. In reality, caring relationships were very much a part of the organizations of the industrial era. Unfortunately, these relationships often formed within groups whose very purpose was based on opposition to the dominant system and the managers who were perceived as running it. The members of these groups often saw themselves as victims of a system that tried to keep them in their place. Managers, on the other hand, viewed caring relationships as a phenomenon that occurred at lower levels of the organization or within the "informal" structure and that it was best to keep them under control.

We should not be surprised that informal groups in which people cared for each other formed under the surface of our bureaucratic organizations of the industrial era. Both history and the human sciences provide evidence that it is natural for the human species to work together and care for each other. What's more, experience bears it out. Later I cite studies that show people actually prefer to work in groups in which people care for each other over groups in which individuals look out for themselves and put the other members down or focus only on the bottom-line profits of the organization and treat people as dispensable resources. Unfortunately, this evidence does not negate the facts of life in the organization, including the fact that in the industrial era we learned to deny our natural drive to work together and to care for each other.

Psychology has taught us that when we deny a drive that we are genetically or socially programmed to pursue, the drive does not go away. Rather, the natural drive resurfaces in another form, often in a different time and place—and frequently in ways that are not necessarily good for us as individuals or as a species. Such is the case with caring relationships. While we were busy trying to prove to ourselves and each other that we didn't need each other or that our emotions should be kept in tow so that they wouldn't interfere with rational decisions, people continued to care for each other behind the scenes. We called these caring relationships *informal* to make certain they were not sanctioned and allowed them to develop only when they did not interfere with the rational goals of the organization.

What Does It Mean to Care?

The spirit of caring to which I keep referring is difficult to describe. It is much like the concept of community. It is more a way of being and living than a concept one can capture in a few short sentences. While trying to define it for myself I ran into more questions than answers— perhaps because the very concept implies a set of paradoxes. Caring implies loving and respecting ourselves as well as others. It requires a commitment both to the individual and to the shared goals of the group. It implies rights but also responsibilities, a nurturing as well as a challenging environment, growth through conflict as well as peace making, belief in the dignity of the person as well as the good of the group as a whole.

As much as we would like it to be so, the spirit of caring is not a feeling or a magical source of energy that emerges just because we agree to love each other or to put our trust in the self-organizing principles of the universe. Caring is a nitty-gritty process that asks those who participate in it to love each other even when others are not very lovable, to make meaning when there is none, to find hope in the face of despair and courage in moments of fear. Indeed, caring sets high moral standards and expects much from those who are part of it. The poignant words of Parker Palmer (1987, p. 20) on community at work are revealing in this matter: "Community is that place where the person you least want to live with always lives. . . . When that person moves away, someone else arises to take his or her place."

My experience tells me that Parker Palmer is right. Caring is not easy when people fail to respond to our caring or when they respond in ways that send a message that our caring is not welcome.

It is much easier to pick and choose those we care for, like innocent children or those who are humble and in need.

But caring demands more than a friendly "hello" or a pat on the back. When we care for our work and each other, we lay ourselves open to claims and responsibilities. This might be the very reason we prefer to run away from caring relationships at work or explain why we choose to hide behind the invisible shield called "the organization" when an issue gets sensitive or people become emotional.

Perhaps the best way to discover what caring communities at work are all about is to observe them. A few years ago I embarked on a search to do just that. I was convinced that people still cared. I looked for groups that might exemplify what it means to love and care for each other as well as their work. Not surprising, I found some. But I didn't find them at the top, where all the noise about shared visions and teamwork is the loudest. Nor did I find them at retreats where a pseudocommunity is manufactured in three days or less and falls apart when the first winds of conflict blow. I found caring work communities where I should have known all along I would find them: in the less formal and often inconspicuous places of the organization where people were working hard to create products and deliver services that would delight their customers; where people were taking time to care for each other; where people were dealing with and learning from the natural conflict that emerges when people are required to work side by side with other people they often never knew before or didn't much care for at first—much like the people who grew vegetables. I also found the spirit of caring alive and well at the fringes of the organization—in union halls, employee clubs, bowling leagues, and at the local chapters of Toastmasters. In short, I discovered caring communities at work wherever I found people working together with their hands and their hearts as well as their heads, holding a life and a task in common.

A Hunger for Caring Relationships

What did I learn from my search? For one thing, I learned that the spirit of caring at work was still very much alive even though it had been driven underground by the forces of rational thinking, destructive power on the part of an executive elite, and our fear of getting too close to each other. Even more revealing, once I worked my way past the small talk and the tough rhetoric, I discovered a hunger for intimacy at work. This discovery shouldn't have surprised me given the fact that hunger is a natural response to being shown something we have been starved of, including caring relationships. People at all levels of the organization told me that they wanted to get closer to their work and each other. Many of them were afraid to try, not only because they were led to believe the system wouldn't let them but also because they weren't sure how and where to start. I found the fear of intimacy notably more intense, though less openly admitted, at the top of the organization, where the art of social distancing had been practiced to perfection. People, especially managers, just didn't know how to deal with the delicate issue of human relationships—or where to turn to get past their fear and learn how to care again.

The issue of relationships at work is particularly troublesome for managers—not only because we are the ones who are expected to fix people problems but also because the system itself places unreasonable demands on managers to fix whatever is wrong. I do not mean to negate the reality that some people appear to revel in the power of their position and use it for destructive purposes. However, several of the managers I talked to felt trapped by the organizational imperative for unlimited growth and profits and locked into a lifestyle created by the very rewards they were given for being loyal and committed. They felt cheated of meaningful relationships at work. It was never written anywhere, they told me, but the implied message was that if you wanted to be a manager you were required to behave rationally and not allow your emotions to get in the way. Some managers were told outright never to get too close to "their people."

Encouraging signs are starting to appear for those who would like to release the power of caring relationships at work. People at all levels of the organization are beginning to speak out about caring. Human relationships at work are getting new press along with concepts such as meaning and spirituality. Indeed, perhaps what we call a search for meaning is really a cry for caring relationships in disguise. Maybe we are beginning to realize that there is no meaning at work or at home without others with whom to share it. Mihaly Csikszentmihalyi, author of several books on discovering meaning and happiness in life, reminds us that the concept of *meaning* itself includes a connection to others as well as to a purpose (Csikszent-mihalyi 1990, 1993). In fact, Csikszentmihalyi's research showed that the caring and confirming feedback of others, whether they be the people with whom we work or the customers we serve, is the very thing that gives work its meaning.

Caring and the Organizational Imperative for Growth

Unfortunately, every message has its shadow side. So it is with the message to make the workplace healthy again. The voices that call caring relationships out from their hiding places in the informal structure of the organization have been muffled by the very programs designed to fix "the organization." In fact, judging by what I heard and experienced, many of these programs were driving relationships at work even farther underground. By reorganizing, reinventing, restructuring, remaking, reengineering, and rewhatevering the organization, without knowing what we were doing we were breaking up work groups that had formed caring work communities. In our efforts to bring teamwork into the workplace, we were interfering with the natural process of relationship building that occurs when people are given the opportunity to work together and care for each other.

Why is it that the organizations of the Industrial Era were so hard on caring relationships in the workplace? Perhaps the answer to this question lies in the nature of organizations themselves. They were created in the first place to provide a place to work. As organizations grew, they took on lives of their own. Eventually, profits became more important than providing work. Some organizations grew to be so big and complicated that the people who worked in them no longer knew why the organizations existed and where they were going. Those in power liked to keep it that way. Many people gave up trying to figure it out along the way. Others swore allegiance to the organizational imperatives for growth and profits at the expense of their own relationships at work and home. In essence, we gave away our work. We granted these huge organizations that we created in the first place to provide work the right to tell us why we should work, when we should work, how we should work, and with whom we should work. What's worse, we became experts at social distancing and mastered the art of protecting ourselves from each other, often killing each others' songs in the process. We did everything we could to control and limit caring relationships at work. In the process we drove the spirit of caring underground, depriving the organization of a powerful source of energy: caring relationships.

Several years ago W. Edwards Deming, often called the father of the quality movement for his work on improving business processes in both Japan and the United States, warned business leaders that they were out of touch with their customers and their employees. What's more, he and others after him warned us that the bureaucratic monster organizations we had created were too costly and inefficient in a world of nimble competitors. Unfortunately, the pressure to produce quarterly earnings forced many leaders to respond to only part of this message—the part about being too costly. They went on cost-cutting rampages. Because labor costs were easy to identify and reductions there could fall quickly to the bottom line, people often were the first to go. Companies laid off workers as if they were unwanted flies at a summer picnic. Processes were reengineered. Entire departments and divisions were eliminated or reorganized. Wall Street loved the short-term results.

Recent efforts by managers and owners of organizations in the United States to reduce costs through massive layoffs have had a devastating impact on human relationships at work that had already been damaged by the rational thinking and the individualism of the industrial era. I argue later that these quick-fix programs delivered the final blow to the already-strained relationship between the individual and the organization. Even programs to introduce teams, an effort that on the surface appeared to promote relationships, often meant that people were required to leave healthy work groups and work on several teams at once while the hierarchy of the organization remained in control. As a customer service manager I interviewed for this book put it: "We are team crazy where I work. People run from team to team like chickens with their heads cut off. In the meantime I lost every friend I had at work."

For several reasons, the message that caring relationships at work are good for people and organizations never got through to the leaders of many organizations. If anything, many of the programs initiated to make organizations more competitive in a global marketplace drove caring relationships even farther underground. While all this was going on, individuals were admonished to stop depending on an entitlement from the organization, grow up, and take control of their own careers. One consultant I know went around telling people to create their own personal corporation called "Me, Inc." Relationships were forced to take the back seat one more time.

Strong Selves Are Made from Caring Relationships

Contrary to what we have been led to believe by some movements within humanistic psychology and the culture of the strong, autonomous individual, an independent self free of intimate relationships is not a strong self. In truth, a strong self is built through strong, healthy relationships. These include relationships to nature, significant others, a personal and social history, special work to do, and special people to do it with. In fact, one of the reasons people feel so frustrated and helpless is that once stable social structures such as the family, the church, the community, and the work group are in transition. People feel as if they have lost something. The something they have lost is their relationships with their work and each other. The words of a friend, whose story I share later, were painfully close to the truth: "I felt abandoned by the organization and my friends; alone and afraid in a world I never made."

As a result of these feelings of alienation and abandonment, people are hungry to belong to someone or something. At times it seems as if anything will do as long as it makes us feel a part of something, including wearing the same clothes, driving the same cars, living similar lifestyles, or believing in the latest spiritual connection to the Universal flow. It is no accident that fundamentalism is on the rise. People are searching for something firm in which to believe and a group to which they feel they belong. When someone comes along with a ready-made answer or an ideology to which we can grab hold, we are eager to embrace it. Any ship is a welcome sight in the middle of a storm.

One of the messages that concerns me in our stormy times is the antientitlement message that says we must take control of our work. Not that it isn't true. Indeed, we must crawl out from the shadows of our organizations and take control of our work. But we must do it together. My fear is that we are making the same mistakes that were made in the industrial era. That is, one more time we are putting all the emphasis on the individual at the expense of our relationships. Like Humpty Dumpty, we are setting ourselves up for a fall. All the king's horses and all the king's men won't be there to pick up the pieces any more than they were the last time we fell.

Robert Bellah and his associates made the point I am attempting to make better than I can (Bellah et al. 1985). Their research suggested that we have moved from an emphasis on "What is in it for me?" (what they call *instrumental* individualism) to how can I develop my self in all of its physical, mental, and spiritual dimensions (what they call *expressive* individualism). The message is still take charge of your life. You don't need anyone. With all the talk about well-rounded and balanced lives, we have yet to realize the power of healthy relationships at work. The emphasis is still on the individual.

Christopher Lasch, author of the aptly titled book, *The Minimal Self*, wrote about the issue of relationships and the strong self (Lasch 1984). He reminds us that a self stripped of its relationships is a beleaguered self concerned only with its own survival. Mihaly Csikszentmihalyi echoes the same theme in his book about the evolution of the self and adds to it the ancient Eastern concept of *harmony*, the idea that autonomous thought and action must be balanced by integrating the individual with nature, other people, and the flow of evolution itself (Csikszentmihalyi 1993). The spiritual writer Frederick Buechner questions whether we can even be human without our relationships (Buechner 1982, p. 46): "You can survive on your own, you can grow on your own, you can even prevail on your own, but you cannot be human on your own." The point is, we need strong, healthy relationships if we are to develop strong, healthy, balanced selves. Indeed, to be human is to be related.

A Time to Care

At some level, we all know that life and work are richer when we care for each other beyond a friendly "hello," a handshake, and a pat on the back. It is no surprise that I discovered caring groups of people at work. It is also no surprise that people are beginning to acknowledge their hunger for more meaningful relationships at work and to speak out about it. People want a more caring experience at work—indeed they prefer a community-like workplace where people aren't afraid to care and show it over a hard, cold, competitive work environment where "bottom line" is all that counts and people are considered expendable. To acknowledge this and talk about it is only the beginning. We must do something about it.

Several managers I encountered while writing this book expressed a strong desire to bring caring relationships out from the informal structure of the organization and into the open where they belong. The problem is they weren't sure how to go about it. They were looking for examples and the support of other caring leaders. That is why I have chosen to write this book in the hope that through sharing my own experiences and the experiences and insights of others who care, we can bring caring relationships out into the open where they have a chance to do their healing work. Before I fall prey to the urge to jump to quick fixes, let's dig a little deeper into the history of relationships at work.

2

Digging Deeper
How We Got Disconnected

It is the corrosive daily frustration, the inability to
communicate or to establish meaningful relationships
that is so soul-shrinking.

> . . . EDWARD T. HALL *Beyond Culture*

Not that many years ago, depending on where you come from,
work, family, and community were connected. This was especially
true in nomadic cultures in which work was part of the everyday
life of the community, but it was also true within pockets of agricultural societies. I recall growing up on a small farm in the 1950s in a
community where the children worked on the farm with their parents, the threshing crews went from farm to farm helping with the
harvest, neighbors gathered at the one-room schoolhouse for the an-
nual Christmas program, the ice cream social at the church drew
more people than the local basketball game, and the social life of
the community was centered on the family. In fact, I grew up in complete ignorance of what a corporation even looked like. My Dad was
a farmer. The organization had little meaning beyond the fact that I

knew that Dad's milk check must come from somewhere. It wasn't until I was out of college that the organization became a very central part of my work and my life.

One of the consequences of the thinking of the Industrial Era, or the "machine age" as historian Lewis Mumford called it, was that the organization was granted permission to take over the role of defining work for many people (Mumford 1963). Mumford reminded us that work gradually became separated from the rest of life. People went off to work in factories, offices, military complexes, schools, hospitals, and anywhere else that could be defined as a place of work. In fact, *work* began to take on a rather narrow definition. For example, staying home and taking care of children or volunteering to help in the community and church was not considered work in the real sense. To qualify as work the activity had to be separated from the family and the community.

Once work became separated from the rest of life, a whole new philosophy developed around people and work. Eventually, the individual became a resource, a cog in the industrial machine. Now and then experts came along to remind those in power that it paid to treat people well, but by this time the worker had been turned into just another resource—and a dispensable one at that. Ultimately, the systems themselves grew so complex that the workers became slaves to the system. The people at the top of the power pyramid weren't free either. Those in so-called powerful positions became slaves to the organization as well as their own status and life-styles, what became known as the "golden handcuffs" (Hagberg 1994).

One of the ironic consequences of the phenomenon of organizational control was that people eventually forgot what their organizations stood for or where they were going. In truth, I believe that the mission, vision craze of the 1970s was a direct response to this loss of purpose and direction. Now here is the irony. We called in consultants who may have been sincere in their desire to help, but they had no sweat equity in the organization and therefore were not connected to the soul of the organization. The end results were missions and visions written from the head that addressed only the task. Caring relationships with our work and each other were not even a part of the discussion.

Early in the twentieth century, critics of individualism and the ideal of progress at all costs spoke out about its consequences for the individual. No one spoke with more passion than the historian and philosopher Lewis Mumford. He dug deep into the origins of the industrial revolution and articulated the events that eventually led to the machine age, making an important point about the nature of people and work along the way. "Men had become mechanical before they perfected machines to express their new bent interests," Mumford wrote (Mumford 1963, p. 3). Mumford was making the important point that with a new era comes a change of mind, "a reorientation of wishes, habits, ideas, goals." Humans had begun to see each other as malleable resources (machines of sorts) long before the great factories of the nineteenth century were built.

In Mumford's view the change of mind that led to the thinking of the industrial era had deep roots that went all the way to the tenth century A.D. and the invention of the clock. People learned to think of time as a commodity, and the clock helped people segment the day into parts. Along with the invention of the clock, new social structures emerged. The Roman army with its highly structured pyramidal hierarchy started a trend that would extend all the way to the modern organization. Eventually the pyramid became the accepted way to structure all organizations.

Mumford pointed out that people did not adapt automatically to the new definition of work as separate from the rest of life. At first, people resisted schedules and job descriptions, working in factories only long enough to supplement their income and return to their farms or their communities. It might have stayed that way were it not for one small thing—the children. Growing up punching clocks in the factories of the early industrial era, children were socialized to think in terms of work as a separate part of life. Time became more linear and compartmentalized into work time and leisure or play time. Eventually even people were broken into segments, not only as individuals who now stood apart from primary groups of family and community but also as persons who could separate parts of themselves. For example, people were encouraged to separate their emotions from rational thinking, their hearts from their heads—a feat we have since discovered is impossible. A society based on the values of individual achievement and rational thinking evolved, and progress was worshipped for the sake of progress. As the well-known commentator Paul Harvey would say, "The rest is history."

Robert Bellah and his associates, who wrote two popular books and several articles about the culture of individualism, are but a few of the current voices calling for a revival of the spirit of community (Bellah et al. 1985, 1992). They traced the justification for individualism and the ethics of progress in the current century to people like John Locke and Adam Smith, who wrote about the moral ideal of progress and believed that if individuals were free to achieve their potential, they would work toward progress in the best interests of the community and the greater social good. But things didn't work out the way they were supposed to. Instead, people fought to get ahead in the organizations of the industrial era, and connections to the community began to fall apart. As for the individual, the freedom sought in such earnest was never realized. The system itself grew to become all-consuming, a living entity that demanded loyalty and commitment from workers. Ironically, even those who succeeded were not free. Their very identities were attached to a role in the organization. They became slaves to a way of life structured on an important title, a fancy house and car, and elaborate vacations that were often as meaningless and hurried as their work lives.

Perhaps the staunch belief in the virtues of civic duty founded in religious traditions had blinded Locke and Smith to the potential that people would ultimately succumb to the imperatives of loyalty to the organization and its growth above all other relationships or that some might look out for their own interests at the expense of others or become addicted to extrinsic rewards and symbols of success and power. Whatever the reasons, the ideal of progress for the good of society was never realized. In fact, ties to the primary groups of family, church, and community were, if anything, loosened by the demands of the organization and the fast pace of a life caught up in the work-and-spend cycle of a mass production, mass consumption society. Eventually one of the few ways left to connect to others was to dress, act, and look alike. In other words, to lead similar lifestyles.

One of the early driving forces behind the ethic of progress and the emphasis on the individual was the assumption that caring relationships cloud rational decision making and stand in the way of organizational and personal success. This idea also goes back a few years. The political philosopher Jean Jacques Rousseau, after observing the privileged corporate entities in eighteenth century France, wrote about the need for the individual to be freed from the constraints of clans, groups, and associations. The great German philosopher Ferdinand Tonnies contributed much to our understanding of the dichotomy between self and society with his concepts of *Gemeinschaft* (community) and *Gesellschaft* (society), later translated by the American anthropologist Robert Redfield as folk society (*Gemeinschaft*) and urban society (*Gesellschaft*). These great thinkers provided a framework for dialogue about the virtues of being attached to a group or community versus individual autonomy and personal achievement long before corporate America entered the debate (Olmsted and Hare 1978).

A common sociologic distinction that emerged from the debate about the self versus society or self versus the organization was to classify some groups as *primary groups* and others as *secondary groups*. Primary groups were viewed as groups in which intimacy, caring, and emotional attachments were welcomed; such groups are the nuclear family, the church, and the community. Secondary groups were believed to form for instrumental purposes. They were considered rational by their nature and consisted of task- or goal-oriented groups, such as the groups that formed in the factories, offices, and classrooms of the modern organization. This dichotomy eventually led to the belief that intimate relationships had no place at work. The debate over when intimacy and caring should be permitted in the workplace and when it should not has been carried on to today.

The separation of the self from the constraints of relationships was an interesting phenomenon in the Western world. On the surface, the separation was most complete inside the large organizations created by the industrial complex. Intimate relationships were forced underground. Organizations were granted permission to manipulate the human resource as they saw fit. The dominant world view pictured the individual as a potentially rational performer in a machine-like (later computer-like) organization. This world view was supported by the managerial-therapeutic thinking of the late industrial era. Efficiency experts followed the advice of scientific management theorists such as Frederick Taylor, who advocated improved working conditions and incentives to induce people to behave rationally, economically, and in ways that contributed to the growth and profits of the organization. The idea was that the individual would benefit from the increased productivity with better products and more leisure time to enjoy them. It also was perceived that loyalty would be rewarded with pay raises, promotions, and a better life. As a result, people developed a false sense of security in the benevolence of the paternalistic organization and the belief that progress would buy happiness. Ironically, now we are told that it's about time we grow up and realize that the age of entitlement is over.

Layoffs and cutbacks are poignant reminders that nothing lasts forever, not even organizations. This may be a blessing in disguise. In truth, organizations may have taken on a life of their own, but they never cared for people. As the great anthropologist Edward Hall reminded us, organizations have no conscience and no heart. They do not care for people. Only people care for people and not as often as they should. It is true that organizations take on a life of their own. By one definition the organization is indeed a living thing. Certainly the organization uses energy from its environment and seeks to grow. The energy comes from the loyal and undivided attention of those who give their life and work to the organization. Organizations might not have a conscience or a heart, but they do want to stay alive and grow. Indeed, they use every bit of energy that they can to do so—even when that means coercing human resources to do more for fewer rewards.

One could argue that the divorce between the self and the organization is now complete given recent large numbers of layoffs and the resultant career uncertainty. The illusion that loyalty to the organization would be repaid with a lifetime career is dead. The age of entitlement is over. We must now grow up and recognize that the organization will not take care of us, if it ever really did. That might be good news. Indeed, the thesis of this book is that the future of our organizations and of our society depends not on the ability of the organization to take care of us but on our ability to relate to and care for each other at work. To put it into a more popular theme, to rekindle the spirit of community at work.

One of the challenges for those who wish to rekindle the spirit of community at work is to better understand the relationship between the self and the organization. This brief review of some of the thinking that dominated the industrial era is merely a start, but it is a reminder that the emphasis on the individual and the manipulation of the human resource discouraged caring relationships at work and forced them underground. It is also a reminder that many people became married to the organization only to discover that the marriage was a one-way contract that turned people into dependent "human resources."

It helps to expose the shadows of our past thinking so that we can embrace them and move on. In the case of relationships at work, understanding how the current relationship between the self and the organization evolved can help us see why it so hard to get close to each other at work—indeed, why we actually *fear* relationships. As the great psychoanalyst Carl Jung asserted, the first step toward healthy change is to embrace the shadows of our behavior. Acceptance of our past errors also helps us discover common ground in our shared humanity. We began to realize that we share not only a common predicament but also a common promise for a better future—one that includes caring relationships at work.

The chapters that follow present a case for rediscovering our common ground as humans who are often alone and afraid in a complicated world we made. When we learn to cultivate this common ground together, uncover the dirt that has accumulated over the years, learn to embrace the shadows and bring relationships out of hiding, we will be well on our way to releasing the power of relationships at work. In the process we will relearn a truth about ourselves voiced by Carl Jung years ago: there is no self without an other. In reality, the self is shaped by our relationships with nature, a shared history, significant others, and meaningful work. Contrary to the thinking of the industrial era, the self is strengthened in its relationship with others and purposes that transcend the fulfillment of immediate personal needs or the needs of the organization to grow and profit at all costs. What's more, there is real power in caring relationships at work.

Earlier in this chapter, I suggested that caring relationships at work did not go away, rather they merely went underground. A closer look at some research that has been around for a long time, if not always appreciated, brings this truth out. The research also reinforces the hope that we can bring caring relationships out into the open, where they belong, and rediscover what it means to care for our work and each other. With that hope in mind, the next chapter takes us back in time to a Western Electric wiring plant in the 1930s and the famous Hawthorne studies.

3

The Hawthorne Revelation

Bad times have a scientific value. . . . We learn geology the
morning after the earthquake.

. . . RALPH WALDO EMERSON

In the late 1920s and early 1930s a group of managers at the Western
Electric Company with the help of social scientists from the Harvard
Business School set out to discover ways to improve worker productivity. This research, known as the Hawthorne studies, named
after the Hawthorne plant in Chicago where they took place, still
have much to tell us about relationships at work. They deserve a
closer look.

The work issue that concerned the management at Western
Electric was the monotony inherent in an assembly job. Earlier studies dealing with the issue of fatigue showed that providing assembly
workers time-out now and then actually increased productivity. The
thinking was that if time-out could reduce the negative effects of
fatigue, perhaps providing incentives for greater output along with
variety in working conditions could reduce worker monotony and
bring about increased productivity. To test their theory, management
with the help of consultants selected a group of six women from the

relay assembly room, where electrical relays were assembled. The group was given a separate work area and improved working conditions, such as better lighting and more space. In addition, incentives were introduced to encourage more output.

The managers at Western Electric and the researchers who worked with them were confronted with an unexpected result. Productivity increased–just as the researchers predicted it would. When the conditions were removed, however, that is, the lighting was reduced, productivity remained high.

The managers and researchers concluded that the special attention had something to do with the increased productivity. After all, they concluded, when there is an effect, there must be a cause. Indeed, for years after these studies were conducted, the phrases *Hawthorne effect* and *halo effect* were used by managers to explain why people perform better under "special" conditions. The human resource movement of the 1960s and 1970s borrowed this concept to promote the special treatment and recognition of employees. Members of this movement believed that paying attention to people, treating them fairly, and providing better working conditions would automatically result in increased productivity.

A second group was observed as part of the Hawthorne studies that confused the managers and researchers even more. This group involved several skilled and semi-skilled men from the bank wiring observation room. The men who worked in this area attached and soldered intricate wiring systems to switchboard components. The skilled and semi-skilled workers were required to work in cooperation. This time the managers and researchers sought to measure a series of wage incentives under the assumption that people are economically rational and would respond positively to an opportunity to make more money.

As it turned out, the workers in the bank wiring room had developed an economic rationale of their own. Perhaps it had something to do with the times. It was the early 1930s and the Great Depression was in full swing. People were lucky to have work. Under these conditions, the men who worked in the bank wiring room had developed an unwritten code that they would protect each other and make certain that everyone had a job. To respond to the incentives and increase output would result in fewer jobs. Thus even under the promise of more pay for increased output, productivity did not rise. The level of production remained steady and so did the number of jobs needed to complete the work. The group had succeeded in their objective to keep everyone employed.

Sociologists Michael Olmsted and Paul Hare provided insight into the findings at the Hawthorne plant (Olmsted and Hare 1978). They suggested that what was revealed in the Hawthorne studies was something different from and more universal than the managers and researchers were realizing at the time. Olmsted and Hare pointed out that it is questionable that the halo effect, so often touted by those who studied the findings, would have sustained the increased productivity of the group from the relay assembly room for the two years they were observed. It certainly does not explain the findings in the bank wiring room. In the opinion of Olmsted and Hare, the managers and researchers had stumbled into something they had not expected to find and may never have fully appreciated—the power of relationships at work. According to Olmsted and Hare, "It seems highly unlikely, however, that lasting increases in productivity could have come about without an additional stimulus. This was provided by the interaction with others in a primary group" (p. 17).

The Hawthorne studies were conducted a long time ago. It would be easy to conclude that they no longer represent what is going on inside the new, more enlightened organization. Yet seasoned managers I know, myself included, have encountered the behaviors observed at Western Electric many times over throughout the years. Some of them have been speaking out and writing books about it. Max Depree and James Autry, both chief executive officers of major companies, are but two executives who have written popular books about the importance of caring relationships at work (Depree 1989; Autry 1991). Other books share stories about the power of caring relationships to transform cultures within the organization. *Team Zebra*, the story of the turnaround of a failing division at Kodak written by business manager Stephen Frangos is an example

(Frangos 1993). These modern-day business leaders have discovered what the managers and researchers discovered at Western Electric years ago. When people are given an opportunity to hold a life and a task in common, to cultivate common ground, a spirit of community will emerge and people will care for their work and each other.

The lessons to be learned from the Hawthorne studies and the stories about caring work environments is that communities at work will emerge even when we try to keep them underground. Inside these community-like groups are codes for defining appropriate behavior (sometimes called *norms*), differentiated roles (including the role of a leader, who is often a different person from the one appointed by the organization), and shared memories. Olmsted and Hare call them informal minisocieties. They can also be called caring communities at work.

Another important discovery that emerged from the Hawthorne studies and other studies like it in the workplace is that communities at work can either promote the goals of the company, as the group in the relay assembly room did, or they can work against the goals of the organization, as did the people who worked in the bank wiring division. Sociologist Edward Shils discovered this paradox when he studied primary groups in the workplace. He called these groups *personal primary groups* to differentiate them from the primordial family. Shils made the crucial point that the personal primary group at work, unlike the primary groups in the village or the neighborhood, often worked against the goals of the greater organization, especially if the organization failed to recognize the relationships within these groups (Shils 1951). In truth, by forcing caring relationships underground, the organization may well have been encouraging a siege mentality that pitted caring groups of people against the uncaring organization.

The discoveries by Shils and others led managers and researchers alike to advocate the control of "primariness" within groups at work. Granted, it was to be expected that some bonding would take place at lower levels of the organization. One could tolerate the coffee club, the Thursday night bowling league, and a little venting now and then in the halls and bathrooms. However, those who wished to demonstrate the "right mind" for being promoted avoided being caught up in these informal gatherings or being identified with those who were too "soft" when it came to human issues. For the most part, workers were expected to restrict intimacy to outside work.

We are our relationships. It is naive to think we can avoid, run away from, deny, or repress relationships. It is also naive, however, to think that caring relationships at work are easy or free of conflict. As organizational communications expert Charles Conrad reminded us, we seldom choose the people with whom we work (Conrad 1985). The reality of life inside the organization is that relationships at work are often unnatural and strained. This is true today more than ever before. The modern workplace in many Western industrialized countries consists of a diverse population—not only because of changes in racial, ethnic, and sex mix but also because people come from different backgrounds and have different world views based on genetic, biologic, and social factors. Work is a place where differences abound. Building healthy relationships requires a willingness to open ourselves up to discover common ground in our differences and a desire to learn from them. Unfortunately, we find it easier to deny or hide our differences behind the invisible shield of the organization and its pervasive need for bottom-line results. As every seasoned manager knows, to open ourselves up to each other is to open up a can of worms. Inside that can of worms are a plethora of problems for which we would rather not be responsible.

Tapping into the power of relationships at work while overcoming the fear that relationships will get in the way of results is an issue most organizations have yet to solve. Yet CEOs, such as Depree and Autry, provide examples that show that when people acknowledge the power of caring relationships and blend personal aspirations with the aspirations and goals of the group and even the organization, results are not adversely affected. On the contrary, organizational cultures that promote caring relationships can contribute to the long-term success of a company. Collins and Porras in their research of companies that consistently weather the storms caused by competitive forces and economic swings noted that trust between leaders and employees was a significant factor that contributed to long-term success (Collins and Porras 1994). Peter Senge spoke to the power of relationships at work when he wrote about companies that have learned to align personal visions with corporate visions and nuture community at work (Senge 1994).

The truth is, building communities at work that respect the integrity of the individual and the group while contributing to the goals of the organization and the common good of a global society will require more than aligning visions. As Parker Palmer reminded us, building community is often a nitty-gritty process that requires the active engagement of people working together discovering a common vision in the midst of differing, at times even conflicting, goals (Palmer 1977). Amitai Etzioni, one of the founders of the modern communitarian movement, clearly reinforced this point when he defined *community* as a place where people go beyond getting to know each other and being nice to each other and accept the responsibility that goes with caring for each other. As Etzioni put it, "Communities speak to us in moral voices. They lay claims on their members" (Etzioni 1993, p. 31).

Perhaps it is the claims that scare us away from caring relationships at work. Or maybe it is the potential for messy human conflict that frightens us. But without claims and responsibilities community lacks the very meaning it is capable of providing. And if we run away from conflict we will never grow. We will never experience the joy of building community together.

Before I close this chapter, let me share a story about community at work that might be a little closer to home. The story takes place in the marketing department of a medium-sized shoe company.

Given what was going on in the shoe industry during the 1980s, it will not surprise you that the marketing department was under a great deal of pressure to develop new products and creative ways to promote them. The normal conflict that goes along with working together was accented by pressures outside the employees' control. To add to their stress, the company had just been "reengineered," resulting in layoffs of several people and an increased workload for those who survived.

The people who worked in the marketing department had always been a "close knit group," as the director, Karen, put it. Consequently, when the layoffs occurred those who remained pitched in to fill the holes left behind. But Karen was also quick to report that the holes left in relationships were never filled. Unfortunately, those left behind had no time to mourn the loss of their friends. The industry was demanding more quality and variety for less money. Large competitors with more brand awareness were forcing the company's products from the shelves of the local stores where it marketed most of the shoes it manufactured.

The changes were taking a toll on relationships within all departments. As one of the employees reflected later, "People were so stressed out they looked for the nearest scapegoat to take out their frustration. Often it was the person working next to them who took the brunt of it."

Karen, the director of the marketing department, was an unusually sensitive person, in many ways a misfit in a highly competitive business. She was also extremely intuitive. She had learned to use both these characteristics to her advantage. For example, Karen was particularly sensitive to the needs of her associates and customers and used this to build strong relationships. Her intuitive skills also helped her develop creative strategies and promotions. Until the reengineering effort came along, Karen had been considered one of the up-and-coming leaders in the company.

The reengineering efforts and layoffs had changed things for Karen. For one thing, she no longer believed that the company and those who made the decisions about its behavior had the best interests of her and her department at heart. One of Karen's best friends from another department had been let go early in the process. Karen's boss, Jim, who had always been a sensitive and compassionate leader, also left, taking advantage of an early retirement option. The new boss was a bottom-line competitor who did not seem to appreciate Karen's efforts at building relationships. On the contrary, Karen was receiving signals that she was "too soft" and needed to spend more time finding ways to cut costs.

Things went from bad to worse for Karen. She was asked to lay off two more people in her department. Karen had a small staff to begin with and knew that the workload for those who remained would be unreasonable. More important, Karen knew and cared for each one of the people in her department. The order to let two more people go put Karen in a terrible dilemma. She was at a loss about what to do.

The people in Karen's department knew that she was in an impossible situation. They also knew how much she cared for them. With the prompting of Joel, who had been in the department since Karen had started thirteen years before, the group decided they would do something to help Karen.

The first thing the department did was to identify the cost savings that would be generated by the reduction of two people. Taking that number as the benchmark for the costs that had to be eliminated, the marketing department began to search for alternative ways to cut costs without adversely effecting the programs that were needed to keep the company competitive. They knew they only had one week to accomplish their seemingly impossible task, because Karen had to respond to her new boss quickly. They worked after hours looking for savings wherever they could identify them.

By the end of a week the people in the marketing department had come up with only half the savings needed to prevent the layoff. They had turned over every stone, including paper usage, advertising agency fees, process flows, and advertising budgets. They had cut so many costs previously there was little room left for additional savings. Then Susan, the newest member of the group, came up with an idea.

"I know that this sounds like a stupid idea, and perhaps a selfish one since I am likely the first one to go," Susan sheepishly began, "but maybe if we all took a cut in pay no one would have to go."

Silence followed Susan's remark. It was Joel who spoke first, but his words came from the heart of the entire group.

"That's a wonderful idea," he replied. And with that, the group quickly calculated how much each person's salary would have to be cut. At the end of their calculations, Susan had another bright idea. "What if we designed an incentive to get the money back based on our ability to outperform our budget?" she asked. "Surely the vice president will listen to a plan that would add profits."

Well, the vice president did not listen to the part about additional incentives, but he did buy into the cost savings and agreed to keep all the people employed providing they exceeded budget. The marketing department accepted the terms, including the pay cuts. No doubt, it was a sacrifice for everyone, but in the collective voice of the group, "It was worth it." Indeed, they later reported that their work took on new meaning and their relationships grew even stronger.

When Karen tells this story she always tells it with a tear in her eye and closes with the same words: "If it weren't for the people I love and work with, I would never have made it through these difficult times. I now truly know the meaning of community at work."

Karen and her department might have been frustrated over their inability to change the minds of those who initiated the layoffs at their company, but they discovered a way around it. What's more, they discovered a sense of community in the middle of it all. However, not every story of our time ends so happily. Maybe that's not the point. Maybe the real point of this and all the other stories about people who care for each other at work is that in the midst of change and the fears that it brings to the surface, being there for each other is the most important thing any of us can do.

Stories like this one remind us that given an opportunity, people will care for each other. Often, caring emerges in the most difficult times, such as the depression era, when the researchers discovered community-like groups at the Hawthorne plant or our current chaotic transition into the information age, in which groups like the marketing department struggle to hold relationships together. Lest we assume that caring is everywhere, we must reflect further and ask ourselves a tough, but essential question: Are we moving closer to our work and each other or are the forces of change driving us even farther apart?

4

The New Organization

A Renewal of Relationships or the Final Blow?

> Even if harsh interventions succeed brilliantly, there is no cause for celebration. There has been some injury. Someone's process has been violated.
>
> *. . . The Tao of Leadership*

Not long ago, I attended a seminar—a popular thing to do these days. This one was on the general topic of change in the workplace and its effect on people. I listened to several speakers talk about the changing paradigms around work and the new social contract between organizations and people.

I have discovered from attending far too many seminars that I often learn as much if not more from the audience than I do from the speakers. On this particular occasion, two themes emerged from listening to the audience. One was that people are confused and overwhelmed by constant change, often expressed as the "program of the week." A second theme that emerged was that if people ever doubted the organization's capacity to care for them as persons, re-cent events had removed that doubt. This audience was pretty clear in their conviction that the organizations had lost any soul they ever had and that most managers were too busy trying to survive the chaos of our time to care for the people who worked for them. Even healthy concepts like teamwork and empowerment were viewed as ways for management to manipulate the human resource. They were perceived as nothing more than fancy words that translated in real life into layoffs and more work with less job security for those left behind. Not surprising, the people who were closest to the products and the customers were the most frustrated. People who worked in plants, on sales teams, or in customer service departments expressed the opinion that what had been introduced to date, under the guise of solid concepts like quality, reengineering, and process improvement, had been administered top down for the sake of the organizational imperative for improved short-term results based on the wisdom of those at the top without checking with those who actually do the work. As they saw it, few leaders in the organization ever really understood the relationships between people and their work, the people with whom they work, and the customers they serve.

In the face of a plethora of programs to fix the organization and improve processes and customer relations through teamwork, this group of people was convinced that morale at work was at an all-time low. In fact, they perceived that many of the programs to introduce quality or to reengineer the corporation were being administered in a way that contradicted the very rhetoric used to promote them. While promoting empowerment of the individual and self-managed teams, top-down programs were being implemented by a hierarchy that insisted people get on board or get out of the way. Some people reported being laid off even after they had worked very hard to show their loyalty by helping to introduce a new program only to discover they were victims of the very programs they initiated. Those who had survived massive layoffs talked about working twice as hard as before, doing their regular work and running from team to team. A seasoned leader in the audience summarized the general feelings well:

Whereas we [the leaders of US corporations] have made progress toward establishing a more competitive position in world markets, we have moved the opposite direction in our relationships with people. Frankly, people don't buy into the message that all these changes are automatically good for them. Whether or not trust in the workplace ever existed in the first place could be debated; nonetheless, people feel that a trust has been broken.

The seminar I attended was not the first time I had heard messages like those described earlier. Others apparently had been picking up these messages as well. The title of an article in the October 24, 1994, issue of *Time* magazine described the issue rather poignantly: "We're #1 . . . And It Hurts." The article described people who had lost their jobs as a result of massive layoffs. Many of them were working at more than one job or at jobs without benefits to make ends meet. Those who were left behind to work for the downsized organizations were forced to work harder and longer hours, often at reduced wages and without benefits, just to keep their jobs.

One of the messages being expressed by those who felt like victims of programs to make the organization more competitive was that transitions like the one we are experiencing in the workplace are far more traumatic to the individual than we might have been led to believe. It is one thing to sit in an executive staff meeting and discuss the implementation plan for the latest program to cut costs and improve productivity, but it is quite another to live through the trauma of losing one's job or watching a friend lose hers and then being asked to work twice as hard as before as if nothing happened.

Unfortunately, the trauma of job loss is only part of the issue. The other part has to do with relationships. People at all levels of the organization are being asked to redefine their relationships—to their work, to the organization, and to each other. People are being forced to leave well-established work groups at the drop of a hat to work on cross-functional teams. This is wonderful for the development of team skills. Furthermore, teams expose people to new experiences that in turn can help them develop new personal skills. The problem with creating teams for teams' sake, however, is that too often those who initiate teams fail to appreciate the impact juggling people around can have on well-established relationships within work groups. We chose to ignore the evidence that roles emerge after a group of people have worked together for a period of several months, sometime years. People were being asked to change roles at the drop of a hat as if people are an exchangeable commodity. In a society that defines who we are by what we do at work and with whom we do it, this is a big deal. A change in our relationships at work implies a change of identity.

For some reason, my mind continued to take me away from the seminar I was attending, this time to a conversation I had had with a friend the previous day. My friend had left the corporate world two years earlier to pursue a career as a consultant. Actually, the choice had been made for him. Like many others I know, he had been laid off—with a nice severance package, mind you. At the time, consulting seemed like the natural thing to do. Things had not worked out as my friend had hoped, however. When I spoke to him, he wanted to connect with a new organization. His comments were revealing: "But I'm not going to go to work for just any company," he said, "I now realize the importance of working with a group of people who care for each other and their work." He added a point for emphasis: "I also know from the depths of my soul the pain of rejection and the true meaning of the poet A. E. Housman's words: 'I, a stranger and afraid, in a world I never made'."

Reflecting on what I was hearing at this seminar and the similar messages I had heard at work, in my classroom, and from the audiences who came to listen to me speak, I realized more than ever that many of the programs initiated to improve quality and make organizations more efficient and competitive had done harm to relationships at work. I recalled the wise counsel of the theologian and philosopher Martin Buber. Buber warned that being rebuked or rejected by those who count in our lives can do great harm to our sense of self and literally kill the human spirit within and between us. On the other hand, Buber continued, the comforting and reassuring words of someone who cares can heal deep wounds and bring out the best in us (Buber 1958). In truth, the encouragement of someone who genuinely cares makes us feel special and confirmed as a unique person. Caring relationships can generate a source of energy that it is impossible to generate on our own.

As I continued to reflect on the messages I was hearing, I realized that in my own life I had witnessed both the negative and the positive power of relationships. I concluded that many of the leaders of our organizations I knew over the years were either ignorant of the power of relationships or knew what they were doing and used this knowledge to increase their own power by denigrating others. Or maybe we were all simply too busy to take the time to care for each other. What a shame if this were true, I thought to myself, especially in times of rapid change when we are all vulnerable to a loss of self identity. Indeed, we need each other more than ever.

As I left the seminar to return to my office, I was bothered by what I had heard and my further reflections on what I had been hearing for a long time. I was convinced that something needed to be done to heal the wounds we had inflicted on each other and our relationships at work before it was too late.

Books have been written about what's wrong with the organization complete with formulas and programs on how to fix it—so many books that one might question the need for another one. Much of what has been written, however, is slanted toward making the organization healthy again. If what I am hearing from people who work in organizations is true, at least some of what has been done in the name of quality, process improvements, and competitive positioning has done more harm than good. The negative impact on the individual and relationships at work caused by short-sighted programs designed to improve processes and cut costs is beginning to show. Even those who not long ago wrote about driving costs out of the system are now admitting that perhaps they overreacted and that relationships and trust are critical to the success of the modern work organization.

At the same time that relationships at work are taking on new emphasis, we are being told that the social contract between the organization and its people is being redefined on new terms. A *Fortune* magazine headline reads "The End of the Job: Business guru, Peter Drucker, writes about the Post-Capitalist Era." John Kotter received substantial press coverage on his book on new rules for survival in the postcorporate age (Kotter 1988). Lester Thurow wrote that the old social contract at work is dead and that loyalty, whether or not it ever meant anything, is a thing of the past (Thurow 1993).

Charles Handy wrote about federated structures that consist of small work groups and a growing segment of workers who are entrepreneurs with portfolios of skills that they offer to multiple organizations. Interestingly, Handy cited trust as a critical factor in an era when relationships are likely to become more distant and people will be expected to relate to more people with whom they share no history (Handy 1994). At the same time, Handy spoke directly to the issue of human relationships. He even suggested that the new workplace should look more like a village where people know and care for each other than the cold structures in which we work today.

To add to the voices of those who announce that the workplace is changing, books about love, caring, and spirituality at work are selling. James Autry mixed love and profits and wrote about the workplace as a new neighborhood (Autry 1991). Authors such as Parker Palmer, Matthew Fox, and David Whyte gave us a new spiritual definition of work as an expression of the human soul (Palmer 1977, 1983; Fox 1994; Whyte 1994). The definition of work itself is being challenged along with the forms for structuring the organization and the social contract between people and the organization.

The truth of the matter is, we have been downplaying the importance of relationships at work for a long time. Until recently, the issue has received little attention. We belittled relationships at work with disparaging phrases such as the "soft stuff" or the "touchy-feely" stuff to avoid dealing with them. Like other issues we would rather avoid, we delegated the responsibility to human resources departments and agreed to go to a seminar on human relationships now and then just to make it look as if we were dealing with the issue. In reality we avoided the claims and responsibilities of intimate relationships as if they were the plague. Even the books and programs designed to transform the workplace took on an "everyone for themselves" quality. Except for the material on teamwork, the issue of relationships—especially relationships between people who share the same workplace for extended periods of time—was mentioned only in passing. Even the material on teams was slanted toward the task. We were often led to conclude that lasting relationships at work were a thing of the past. People were expected to take responsibility for their own work while running from team to team at the drop of a hat. It is no wonder we are confused when we are now told that relationships are important and that we must learn to trust each other.

We are being told by experts and politicians that we must grow up and stop relying on the organization or big government to take care of us. The age of entitlement is over, they say. We must learn to take personal responsibility for ourselves, our work, and our career. We must create "Me, Inc." There is truth in these warnings, but I am not at all certain that the human species is ready to throw out meaningful and lasting relationships at work. In fact, we are making the same mistake we made in the industrial era. Overemphasis on the individual at the expense of relationships and strong community ties has left us vulnerable to control by the state and the organization. Before we knew what had happened we were dependent on the organization for work. Indeed, we gave the organization permission to define our work for us—and our relationships at work along with it. We should have learned our lesson the first time. To shine in our work we need meaningful work, but we also need meaningful relationships with each other. The two are connected. In other words, we need our work, but we also need each other, people we can count on, people with whom we can share our work and receive the feedback that tells us that our work counts for something. We need to be confirmed by others who count in our lives.

Relationships at work have always been important. The psychoanalyst Carl Jung reminds us that healthy relationships are what the self is made of and that we build a stronger self by connecting with others (De Laslzo 1959), a point of irony given our emphasis on the autonomous individual and our obsession with self in the past few decades. We have been busy discovering, developing, fulfilling, actualizing, and doing whatever else is needed or in vogue to find and improve upon the self. In our efforts to discover our "true selves," we have not been paying much attention to our relationships with others. This is especially true at work. Inside our large organizations relationships have been downplayed, denied, or neglected for a long time. We listened too well to the call of the organization for strong, autonomous, totally rational individuals who were in need of no one. When things began to fall apart and we needed each other the most, we weren't there for each other. We had become experts at distancing ourselves from caring relationships. To complicate matters even more, the stress of the times has forced people to focus on their personal needs or to work twice as hard simply to survive. We have no time left over for each other.

When we neglected our relationships or, worse still, drove them underground, we paid a huge price. We encouraged the pitting of management against the workers. Often the caring communities that did form—and form they did in spite of our efforts to squelch them—shaped their identities around a subversive attitude toward a management they believed did not care for them or their work other than raw output. When this happens, the organization loses the power generated by groups of people who care for each other and their work. But that is exactly what we have been doing. Over the years, we have been driving relationships underground. We became experts and specialists who were often far removed from our products and customers. We lost the power that comes from connecting who we are to what we do in spiritual ways and then linking our work to others for whom we care and who care for us in return. This is what people like W. Edwards Deming, the father of the quality movement, were telling us over a decade ago. The problem in America is that people became disconnected from their work, their customers, the organizations they worked for, and the people with whom they worked—and not necessarily in that order. We were simply showing up to do a job or to build a career.

One of the reasons I chose to write this book is that I believe we need healthy relationships at work—and we need them now more than ever. We are possibly in the middle of one of the most traumatic transitions in the history of humankind. Nowhere is this felt more than in the workplace. The meaning of work itself is being redefined along with the social contract between people and the organizations they serve. As is often the case in times of transition, experts are full of advice. Some of them tell us to reengineer our way to profitability; others admonish us to take personal responsibility for our work and to develop ourselves mentally, physically, emotionally, and spiritually. Still others point to the self-organizing principles in the natural forces of evolution and the need for values, visions, and relationships. At times, the advice is so plentiful and overwhelming that we feel like crying out: "Enough, already!"

Poets and philosophers have reminded us over the years that times of adversity and chaos either can bring us together to form common bonds that make us stronger or can pull us apart to be cast into a sea of confusion and blame where finding scapegoats seems to be the only way out. It has also been said that in times of transition we need each other the most. Ironically, we often run the other way. Therefore, the real challenge in these times is to find ways to keep us from falling apart—inside ourselves as we struggle to find meaning and make sense of it all and outside ourselves as we seek to connect to others.

If we are going to survive these times and build healthier places to work, we need to discover new ways to work together. This means we will need to bring relationships out of hiding and into the open where they belong. To put this metaphorically, we must discover common ground, begin to cultivate it together. We must turn over the soil that has been trampled by the feet of those who persuaded us that loving and caring at work were not good for us and release the power of relationships at work. While cultivating the ground together we will rediscover the joy of loving, caring, and working together that we have lost over the years.

Before I close this part of the book, I must share two stories. The first is about a threshing crew in the 1940s and a little boy who learns what community at work is all about. The second story is about an executive in the 1990s who faces a difficult assignment. In the process of carrying out his mission he makes the mistake of getting to know and care for the people he has been asked to lay off. As a result, he is unable to complete his mission. In the midst of it all, however, he also discovers the real meaning of community at work. One story concerns the 1940s, the other the 1990s, but the lessons they hold are the same. The most important lesson of all is that community is about a conscious commitment to care for our work and each other. To quote the words of my dear friend and spiritual leader, James Frank Mossman, "Community, whether real or virtual, requires a conscious commitment to holding a life and a task in common."

The first story was written by James Mossman. I was moved the first time I read the story, partly because of its touching nature, but more because it touched a special spot in my own heart because I had a similar experience as a boy growing up on a small farm in Wisconsin. I was tempted to rewrite the story into my own experience, but I decided instead to modify the story slightly to reflect my own experience while maintaining the integrity of the original. I hope I have accomplished that.

The Harvest

James Frank Mossman

In 1941, 1942, and 1943 most able bodied men of rural west central Minnesota, like the rest of the country, were off to the humid jungles of the Pacific or the gritty air of the North African deserts to fight the second great war of the century.

Back home, the crops still needed to be planted, cultivated and harvested. So the old and young were recruited to get the job done.

Electricity and the REA [Rural Electrification Administration] had not yet come to Grey Eagle, Minnesota, nor had indoor plumbing, combines, and rubber-tired tractors. Harvest time consisted of a gathered community called the threshing crew. This core community moved from farm to farm. New faces were added at each farm to provide the resources needed to get the wheat and oats, barley and flax off the land and into commodities for conversion into food and drink, oil and cloth.

We didn't know it then, but what we put together at threshing time was a virtual community with a life and task in common. This task of the harvest and its community of workers living a life in common for this short time knit and weaved the community together, for good or ill.

This virtual community blossomed or wilted as a direct influence of several dynamics that even in this day of cyber electronics, Internet, Jacuzzis (indoor or out), and tractors as luxurious as fine cars cause a community, virtual or real, to flourish productively or to disintegrate. If the dynamics are negative and disintegration results, then people, product, and profit all are hurt.

I'll come back to this point and try to glean the grain of these dynamics from the chaff, but first let me tell my story.

I visited "the farm" often in my early years. My father had been part owner prior to his death and my mother still owned his share and needed to look out for the investment. My sister and I had played there often and had fun. I had been there at harvest time before and visited the fields with my Aunt Gertie to deliver the morning and afternoon sandwiches and drink to the men.

But 1941 was a special year. As a ten-year-old, I was given a team and a wagon of my own. Like the men, I would collect the bundles of grain and haul them from the field to the feeder belt of the steam-driven threshing machine. Each farm had to provide a certain amount of "man power." Because several of the able bodied were overseas fighting the war, I was now part of the threshing crew. Fortunately I was big for a ten-year-old.

Being part of the threshing crew seemed to be the natural and "right" thing to do. After all, Dad had been part owner of the farm. It was only right that I pick up the load. It was my duty to do so. However, I never saw being part of the threshing crew as my duty. On the contrary, I was elated and proud as a peacock to be one of "the men." A right of passage had been reached. I no longer would be forced to ride with Aunt Gertie in the old pickup truck to bring morning and afternoon food and drink. I had a team and a wagon of my own!

Maude and Bert, the big bay Belgians would do as I told them—so I hoped. I would sit at the table, breakfast, noon, and supper with the men and drink coffee, laced with milk, from a saucer.

The night before the harvest began, I hardly slept at all. My mother had dropped me off at the farm the day before. I had watched with awe and much trepidation the core community proceed like a parade of machine and engine, teams and wagon, trucks and cars, down the road, turning at the farm and then into the field to assemble.

I was scared and shy. I went to the barn where Uncle Fred had shown me the stalls that housed Maude and Bert and the harnesses that hung on the wall like heavy weights. The horses were so big, much bigger than I remembered them. I didn't know how I was going to bring the heavy harnesses from the wall to the backs of these huge animals. They made my pet horse, Morgan, look tiny. I was even more discouraged when I discovered that Uncle Fred would be no help. He had retired to the hayloft with his bottle.

Just then, Alvin's voice rang out, "Pretty big, huh kid. Here, let me show you how that harness goes. That's a dandy team. They won't give you any trouble, but I'll help you hitch them in the morning—that is, if you want me to."

Oh yes! I wanted—*badly.*

Saviors come in all sizes, shapes—and odors. Even the smell of manure on Alvin's boots could not mask the message of grace in his kind words.

The day of the harvest broke with a clear sky and warm temperatures. It was already 70 degrees at six A.M. When I arrived at the barn Alvin was there true to his word. He had already hitched his own team. He proceeded to help me harness Maude and Bert. He was careful not to do it *for* me, but instead coached me so that I felt like I did it myself. His method proved effective, for during the days that followed Alvin complimented me several times. And each time I knew it was real since he had let me struggle and learn on my own. Maude and Bert, on the other hand, were less complimentary, and I was certain that I saw them smiling in jest at me more than once as I struggled with the harness.

Nineteen forty-one was a good year for the harvest. A healthy community emerged around the threshing crew of men and women. Good humor was abundant. People helped each other. Under Alvin's kind and watchful eye I worked and learned much. I probably loaded only one wagon to his three, but he never once put me down. Instead he would offer helpful advice like: "Maybe if you balance the load a little over here it would ride tighter." Alvin also helped me in the social dimension of the harvest. He presented me to the men in a way that made them accept me in spite of my youth. When someone would start to ridicule me, he would intervene and steer the subject in a different direction. When I was the last one in at night he would wait for me and help me pitch the remaining bundles from my wagon.

Yes, '41 was a good year. Aunt Kate and Uncle Fred were pleased with the harvest. The grain was clean and consequently brought a good price, and the great gray threshing machine never broke down, not even once, keeping overhead low.

The week ended on a note of celebration and the community of threshers moved on to the next farm to function again as a community with a life and task in common, but with some new and different players.

The harvest of '42 was a different story. At first, things appeared the same. The community gathered in the same way with the same parade of men and machines traveling down the gravel road to the same fields. But that's where the similarities ended.

I had been looking forward to the harvest, expecting the same caring community to welcome me with Alvin's help. But when I looked for Alvin he was nowhere to be found. Eventually, I learned that he had died from a lightening strike while in his hay field in June. I felt scared, empty, and lonely. I was certain that someone would come to my rescue, as Alvin had the year before. I asked the first man I saw for help with the heavy harness so that I could oil it in preparation for the following day. He glared at me and began to curse, "What the hell, kid. Can't you pull your own? Little shits like you oughten be here, anyway. All you do is get in the way and slow things down. Why don't you go play with the girls?"

The next day, the day of the harvest, began with a gray, misty dawn. I overslept. Quickly, I dressed and hurried off toward the barn. I stumbled and fell in front of the open barn door. Some men were gathered there, already drinking beer. They laughed at my muddy clothes and my efforts to pull the harness from the wall. "What you gonna do, wash the grain," they teased. "You so stupid you don't know you can't thresh in the rain. You must be the dumbest kid that ever lived."

I felt totally humiliated. I wanted to hide. I left the barn and walked the path past the house where some men were eating, past the ice house, and into the old apple orchard. I sat down to contemplate what I had done to lose the respect of the men. Surely, I must have done something terribly wrong. After a while, I returned to the barn. I brushed Maude and Bert and tried to talk to them.

That day dropped from bad to worse. A couple of fights broke out between the men, for what reason I had no idea. No one talked to me. I looked for Uncle Fred, but he had taken off for town to buy some more beer. When I finally found him, he was snoring in the hayloft and smelled like a brewery.

The day ended with a ray of hope as the sun set beneath the clouds in a big orange ball, a harbinger that tomorrow would be clear.

The morning of the second day of the harvest I was up early. I had Maude and Bert positioned in the alley of the barn before most of the men had even arrived. One of the men grabbed his horses by the halter and pulled them out into the alley, yelling at me to "get the hell outta the way." Another man swatted me across the back with his pitch fork and poked at Maude and Bert. By the time we all left for the fields with our teams, Maude and Bert were jittery, and I was fighting tears away between spurts of anger.

Things did not get any better in the fields. I worked hard all morning but produced only two partial loads to show for it. My attention was pulled away from my work toward the men who had berated me. I could only think about how I might get back at them.

By the time I delivered my second load to the feeder belt, the big gray threshing machine had broken down. The grain was dirty as a result of using the wrong screens. The blame ran rampant. There was shouting and chaos.

As we ate lunch I stared at the men who sat sullen at the picnic table. No one was talking. I wondered where the humor and good spirit of the year before had gone.

My third load was a disaster and produced what turned out to be the frosting on the cake of my bad day. In the stress of the day I had forgotten the lesson Alvin had taught me about balancing my load. My wagon tipped, spilling bundles of grain all over the gravel driveway. Maude and Bert stumbled briefly, then stood patiently waiting. And patience was indeed needed. The tongue of the wagon had been broken beyond repair. I freed Maude and Bert by releasing the linchpin that held them to the wagon and watched them drift off to graze in the pasture.

One of the men approached me. He planted his face in front of mine so close that I could feel his smelly breath on my lips. "What the hell is the matter with you! Get the hell outta here and take those glue factory plugs with you."

I left the field, my head hanging toward the ground.

I tried to find Uncle Fred, but he was drunk and loud and arguing with his accusers. Eventually I found Aunt Emma. She put her arm around me. I felt rescued at last.

The following day half the men and teams were gone. By week's end the big gray threshing machine moved to the next farm where there was ripe grain to be harvested. Ripened grain does not wait for even dysfunctional communities to heal. At the Mossman farm, grain still stood in shocks in the field.

That year, there was no celebration. There was nothing to celebrate except the relief of tension as the dysfunctional community disbanded. There had been no task and a life in common. The product we produced was as bad as the morale of the workers. As for me, I never wanted to thresh oats again.

In spite of, or maybe because of, my bad experience in 1942, I learned some things about community from my two years as a member of the threshing crew. For one thing, I learned that community, whether real or virtual, is about people making a conscious commitment to holding a life and a task in common. If that commitment is lacking, the community falls apart. I also learned that attention must be paid to morale. Furthermore, mentors need to help the young and inexperienced. Without mentors the community ceases to be a learning community and productivity suffers. And it's not enough to talk community. One must walk the talk and show by his or her behavior a willingness to care for the task and the people. I learned that it is important for each person to understand his or her role and to be valued for performing it. Most of all, one must know that help, not hell, is on the way when things go wrong, as they are bound to in an imperfect world.

The second story is about a sensitive executive who struggled with a difficult assignment but in the middle of his struggle discovered the joy of community at work. I call him John, although that is not his real name.

The Closing of a Division

John worked for a large food company. The company was going through a reengineering process. As part of the process, each division was evaluated for its current performance and future potential. The custom packaging division was one of three divisions that did not pass the test. Management concluded that the division was not producing the results expected of them and probably wouldn't in the near future. The decision was made to shut down the division, close the facilities, and lay off the one hundred and twenty people who worked there, with a very fair severance package, of course. John, a middle-aged manager who had been with the company for twenty-five years, was given the difficult assignment of carrying out the plan. His assignment translated into a month at the facilities learning everything he could about the division and particularly the customers, so that the effects of the closing on the customers who might be doing business with the other divisions would be minimized, and then announcing the closing and subsequent layoffs.

John did not feel good about his assignment. He knew in his heart that this was not a good fit for him. For one thing, he hadn't managed a large group of people for years, particularly line people who worked in plants and with customers. Even in the days when he had direct line responsibility, he had been more of a relationship builder. He knew that this assignment called for a thick skin and an ability to hold one's emotions in check. Though he had learned to play the unemotional game of bottom-line business well over the years, he wasn't certain that he could do it anymore. But he had always been a loyal employee. Furthermore, as he readily admits when he looks back on the experience, he was afraid of losing his own job. Thus, John accepted his new assignment—a decision that proved to have a profound impact on his job and his life.

The plane ride to his new assignment gave John time to reflect. He remembered how he had fallen into a career in business, more by default than intention. His adolescent dreams were to become a preacher or a college professor like his older brother. But the rigor and discipline of studenting didn't fit back then. So like his father before him, John had thrown himself into other roles: husband, father, and breadwinner. Early in his career John had learned to adapt the qualities and skills that he would have applied to preaching and teaching to the roles of supervisor and manager. In fact, as he reflected now, those were the very skills that had served him well in those early days. A smile crossed his face as he recalled the customer service groups he had worked with as a supervisor in the late 1960s and early 1970s, the marketing group he managed as his career blossomed, and finally, the division of which he had been placed in charge. John liked to think he had inspired the division to become the most profitable in the company. "How had such an overly sensitive misfit as I succeeded in the competitive world of business?" he asked himself as the pilot announced that Nashville, Tennessee, was now visible to the right side of the aircraft.

As John continued to reflect on his unlikely rise to corporate stardom, he chuckled. In his heart he knew that he had merely done what he had to do to survive along the way. Out of knowing nothing better, he had built relationships between people, helped them see a goal for themselves and the group, and dared to be there for them when they needed him. He also recalled how at times his willingness to become entangled in people's lives caused him frustration. "Perhaps I was just lucky," he concluded.

About this time, John's mind shifted to his current role in the organization, that of corporate vice president of planning. How far he had come from those early days of struggling his way through the demeaning role of customer service representative, spending sleepless nights as a supervisor and later a general manager worrying about whether he would be able to help two people steeped in conflict ever see their way through it, dealing with irate customers who just needed someone to be the target for their venting. John remembered the day he had accepted the promotion to a corporate role and how far removed from the joy and the frustration of everyday interaction of people, products, and customers he had traveled. He remembered a consultant he had heard not long ago call this "dumb-upness" and define it as "the higher you go the more disconnected and consequently the dumber you get."

But all that was history now. John knew that he had a tough job to do, like it or not. As the plane landed, he set his jaw and his mind to the task ahead of him.

It did not take long for John to recognize that he was not welcome at the custom packaging division. Even after taking into consideration the natural suspicions of Al, the general manager, and his staff over the intrusion of an outsider—especially one from corporate—John still felt that his reception was unusually cool. He sensed that Al knew his visit was more than a part of a new program to reacquaint top management with the real world at the plant level, which is the message that corporate had delivered. More than ever, John was bound and determined to complete his assignment as quickly as possible and get back to the more benign role of corporate planner.

The first few days at the custom packaging division were tough ones. Everyone avoided John like the plague. On several occasions, John reached for his best interpersonal skills in an effort to start a dialogue with someone. Eventually, the office manager, Julie, began to share bits and pieces of what was going on, and a clearer picture started to take shape.

As a result of his talks with Julie, John learned that business had started to go downhill for the division right after Pete, the previous general manager who had been with the division for over thirty years, retired. Julie pointed out that Pete had been a relationship builder who cared about everyone who worked there. "After Pete left, and the new management came in with their quality programs and process improvement efforts, which people soon learned translated to cutting costs in the form of people, morale went down hill," she confided. John recalled when this had happened and how corporate had blamed Pete for leading the business into its current dilemma by not watching costs and by being too attached to his people. The truth was, however, that up until the time of Pete's retirement the region had been doing quite well.

Over the next two weeks John made a fatal error—at least fatal to the task he was assigned. He took the time to get to know the people at the custom packaging division. Soon he discovered that

Susan, the manager of information systems, was the mother of two blossoming boys, ages five and seven, who loved to go to the zoo with their mom and dad. He also learned that her agreement with Pete three years ago to work part-time had later been revoked by Al, mostly because of the cutbacks in the department. "We are changing to new PCs," Susan informed John, "and there is so much work and so few people to get it done."

Next, there was Troy, the plant manager. John learned that Troy loved to referee high school basketball. Tracy, the sales manager, shared with John that she was writing a book about spirituality in the workplace. She was the one to tell him about the loss of two large customers. Tracy blamed the loss on poor service and low employee morale, which she noticed had deteriorated dramatically after the fifteen percent staff reduction. Before he knew what was happening to him, John was back in his own division learning about people and trying to find ways for them to find joy and meaning in their work and their relationships with each other. "What am I doing?" he asked himself, "I'll never be able to carry out this dreaded assignment if I let myself get close to these people."

To use an old cliché and make a long story short in the same sentence, John was not able to carry out his assignment—at least not as planned. Instead, he quit his job and worked with the staff of the custom packaging division to write a new business plan. The division presented the plan to a local bank, which agreed to help them fund an employee buyout of the division. The last that was heard, the division, renamed the Packages for People Company, had regained the customers it had lost and was doing very well in a market niche for natural foods.

As for John, he stayed on as a consultant to the division and eventually built a business on helping people build healthier relationships at work. His friends say that he appears to be busy, and although John admits life is not perfect by any means, nonetheless he is happy doing what he loves best: building relationships at work. He often refers to the incident with the custom packaging division as the closing of a division and the opening of a company. What's more, as John often says with a great deal of pride, the new company was not the only grand opening. The aborted mission to close the custom packaging division was a grand opening of a life that needed new energy: his own. It was also a lesson in the true meaning of community at work, not only for John but also for all the people who worked in the custom packaging division who learned that caring for their work and each other is what community is all about.

II

Bringing Relationships into the Open

If the physics of our universe is revealing the primacy
of relationships, is it any wonder that we are beginning
to reconfigure our ideas about management in
relational terms?

. . . MARGARET WHEATLEY
Leadership and the New Science

5

Four Reasons to Care

Grandpa said back before his time "kin folks" meant any
folks that you understood and had an understanding with, so
it meant "loved folks." But people got selfish, and brought it
down to mean just blood relatives; but that actually it was never
meant to mean that.

> . . . FORREST CARTER *The Education of Little Tree*

Thus, we can learn that the ethic of sharing is not "unnatural"
and try to revive it even though we dwell among nonrelatives.

> . . . MELVIN KONNER *The Tangled Wing*

As hard as we tried to deny and suppress caring relationships at
work, they never went away, at least not completely. The revelation
in the Hawthorne studies was that people were caring for each other
inside the large organizations of the industrial era in spite of the
efforts to separate our heads from our hearts. We may have driven
them underground for a while, but that didn't stop people from caring for each other. In reality, people still formed community-like
groups that shared a life and a task in common, though they were
informal and often hidden from the view of those who were in

power. From this, one might conclude that caring relationships are natural for the human species—even at work. Or at least we can conclude that relationships will form even when we try to suppress them. There must be a reason for this. In other words, caring relationships must make sense at some level.

Contrary to what we have been taught, relationships are not an option. They are part of who we are. We can attempt to escape them or deny their existence, but they are still a part of us. Even when we think we are alone in the solace of a remote cabin or an empty office, we find ourselves reflecting on our relationships and carrying on conversations in our heads with the significant people in our lives who have shaped our sense of self, our picture of who we are. The anthropologist Gregory Bateson postulated that we think in stories complete with significant characters from our past, present, and future lives (Bateson 1979). We carry our scripts, and thus our relationships, with us wherever we go. The point is, relationships are not optional. They are part of who we are whether we like or not.

Accepting the idea that relationships are part of who we are is a step in the right direction, but it doesn't take us far enough. If we are going to tap into the power of relationships at work and learn from our differences, we must take another step. We must build relationships based on openness and trust. And this will happen only if we dare to get close to each other in the spirit of empathy, expose parts of ourselves to each other, and discover common ground in the process. In other words, we need to let go of our self-protection rituals long enough to get to know each other and learn to appreciate our common humanity. We must bring caring relationships out into the open.

As difficult as it might seem, learning to care for each other is not unnatural for humans. Indeed, in this chapter and the two that follow it I attempt to show that caring for each other at work is not only natural but also good for us as individuals and as a society as a whole.

I can think of four reasons to care for each other. The first reason is a practical one. Caring is good for us. In fact, it is natural to the human species. Evidence from the history of our species shows that given the option to care for each other or to treat each other with total disregard, we will frequently choose to care for each other, notwithstanding the fact that it usually takes more than one caring person and a strong leader to pull it off. The Hawthorne studies (see chapter 3) provide evidence that caring relationships even thrived in the rational atmosphere of the machine-like industrial organization.

The second reason for caring for each other is that caring is contagious. If enough people do it, it catches on and becomes a way of life. A very rewarding one, I might add. People who work in groups that care for their work and each other report less stress and more joy in their work.

The third reason for caring is that it generates a power of its own. This power can be a source of energy for the individual as well as the organization. In truth, a strong self is built through strong relationships with significant others and the confirmation of people who count in our lives. Therefore, people who work in organizations and institutions with caring cultures are empowered to create quality products and services that meet the needs of discerning customers. In other words, caring relationships are a powerful source of energy for the organization as well as the individual.

The fourth reason for caring relationships at work is that they make work more fun. This point may sound simple and trite, but it is every bit as important as the other three reasons for caring. Indeed, having fun with each other while working together might be one of the biggest reasons relationships are so powerful. Anthropologist Edward Hall reminded us that humans along with several other species learn through play and what we call "having fun" (Hall 1976). In making this point, I cite the work of the Dutch historian Johann Huisinga, who proposed the provocative theory that all human institutions started with a group of people having fun together. Perhaps this is the very point Jack Stack tried to make (with much success, I might add) in his book, *The Great Game of Business* (Stack 1992). I discuss that later. First I elaborate on the four reasons mentioned earlier.

Caring Is Good for Us

One of the quotations at the beginning of this chapter comes from Melvin Konner's book: *The Tangled Wing: Biological Constraints on the Human Spirit* (Konner 1987). Konner reviewed from the perspective of one who is both a biologist and an anthropologist the biologic reasons for human behavior, including the limits on our capability to care for ourselves and each other. Konner looked at human behavior from the broad perspective of primitive and modern cultures. He concluded that in spite of all the terrible things we have done to each other over the years, a value for human relationships and an ethic of sharing is a common thread woven into the history of the human species. In other words, Konners suggested that caring is natural to the human species.

Evolutionary psychologist Robert Wright, author of the popular book *The Moral Animal* also suggested that the human species is naturally inclined to care—and for good reason (Wright 1994). Species that care for others of their kind last longer. In other words, the best way to compete for long-term survival is to cooperate. Not only is it good for the species in that reciprocal caring increases the chances that a group will stick together in time of need, but also it benefits the individual. The simple truth is, people who treat other people with respect usually get respect in return. Thus from the perspective of evolutionary psychology, caring makes good sense. Species the members of which learn to care for each other are likely to be around longer than species that do not.

Mihaly Csikszentmihalyi writes about the evolution of "the self." Like Wright, Csikszentmihalyi suggested that caring is programmed into the human species. He put it like this: "Thus we are all descended from extroverted ancestors—the survivors—and our brains are wired to experience pleasure when being with others (Csikszentmihalyi 1993, p. 45).

The practical reasons for caring go beyond the individual. Studies in game theory conducted by Robert Axelrod, an American political scientist, demonstrated that "reciprocal altruism" (treating others well so that one is treated well in return) is a natural development in human interaction (Axelrod 1984). Axelrod observed more than 200 participants in a computerized version of the game of "prisoner's dilemma," wherein the players could actually record and remember behavior that led to the mutual benefit of all participants. He concluded that people will indeed gravitate toward "give and take" behavior (Wright calls it "tit for tat"; it is also commonly referred to as "one good turn deserves another"). It is as if the human species has learned that when people and groups cooperate for the good of all or most, they will not only ensure the survival of the species but also get more done and produce better quality. From this one might conclude that if people can actually see the outcomes of their behavior, they will choose to cooperate, which leads me to my second point.

Caring Is Contagious

Robert Wright also points out that caring is contagious. Studies with small groups validate this point and show that whereas one caring individual might have a difficult time changing a group in which caring is discouraged, two or more people who care can have a substantive impact (Borman 1990). Once caring becomes a way of life, it is difficult to change, as the group in the bank wiring room at Western Electric demonstrated. To use Wright's words, "Even if several steadfast noncooperatives arrive on the scene at once, they still can't subvert a population of TIT FOR TATs. Simple, conditional cooperation is more infectious than unmitigated meanness" (Wright 1994, p. 200).

Studies show that groups of people who care for each other accomplish more over the long haul. *Team Zebra* by Stephen Frangos tells the story of the turnaround in the black-and-white division of Kodak (Frangos 1993). The caring relationships between members of the team were an important factor in their ability to achieve phenomenal results. The very popular book *Zap! The Lightening of Empowerment* by William Byham put caring relationships at the center of what is needed for healthy, productive work groups (Byham 1988). Hirotaka Takeuchi, author of *The Knowledge-Creating Company*, presented a strong case for the power of relationships to create knowledge (Takeuchi 1996). He pointed out that companies in Japan tap into the *tacit* knowledge embedded in relationships, whereas US companies tap into the hard facts or *explicit* knowledge. The secret, according to Takeuchi, is to marry the two to create knowledge and store it in the memory of the organization. Later, I share more stories, including one from my own experiences with a division that adopted the theme "We Care" and became one of the most successful divisions in a large company to make this point. For now, it is enough to point out that leaders and experts alike are beginning to recognize that caring relationships at work are an essential part of a learning, thus creative, work environment.

In summary, evidence from the field of evolutionary psychology and studies within small groups in and out of the workplace demonstrate that humans have the capability to use each other merely for personal gain but that we also have the capability to love and care for each other. Moreover, when presented with a choice, we often choose to cooperate with each other for the common good of the species. This is especially true when we are given the opportunity to see and understand the consequences of our behavior and the support of others who care, most of all our leaders. In other words, given the choice, a personal awareness of the consequences of our behavior, and the support of leaders who care, we frequently choose to cooperate. Why? Because it is to the personal benefit of the individual and the survival of the species to care for each other.

Caring Generates a Power of Its Own

There is another, more difficult to articulate reason for caring that leads me to conclude that caring makes sense for the individual as well as the group and the organization itself. Caring for each other is powerful stuff. Caring relationships between people who share a common work goal actually produce energy. It is an energy force that is difficult to describe in practical terms. It is activated when people share common ground, let go of their egos, push cultural barriers aside, and really care for each other. Perhaps it can only be understood through experience and communicated through the language of metaphors and analogies.

One way to understand the positive energy produced by caring relationships is to observe the opposite. That is, to experience the negative energy caused by bad relationships. Physicist David Bohm, one of the leaders in applying quantum physics to human relationships, made this point when he referred to the interrelatedness of all objects by using an example of people who experience conflict (Bohm 1980). If one person takes on another, all those who observe the incident are affected. Most likely you have experienced this first hand. One of the students in my class who worked in a particularly dysfunctional group said it best, "I could cut the tension with a knife." In other words, when a relationship between two or more people is out of sorts, everyone in the group feels it in the form of negative energy. It follows that the opposite is also true. When people care for each other and confirm each other, a positive energy is released.

As noted earlier, the role of healthy relationships at work has been receiving new press. But the power of relationships is not a new discovery. Experts in the field of sociology and psychology have preached for years that, contrary to what we were led to believe by those who preached the ethic of individualism and persuaded us that the autonomous self is an island onto itself, a strong self is built through connections to a history, a place, and strong, lasting relationships with significant others. One of the early proponents of this view was the sociologist George Herbert Mead, who along with others from the University of Chicago proposed that our first glimpse of our "self" is through the eyes of a significant other, usually a parent (Mead 1967). Other social scientists expanded on Mead's work, but they all emphasized the concept that we learn about ourselves and take on an identity by "taking the role of the other." In this view, the self is a social concept that is shaped and reshaped by acting on and receiving input from its environment, especially its relationship with others. The old cliché there is no *me* without *you* is far more true to life than we might have thought.

Several years ago the power of relationships was brought home for me in a brief talk given by a wise leader with years of experience. The title of his talk was "It's Not *What* You Know, but

Whom You Know That Counts." Playing off a twist of irony, the speaker proceeded to build a case for the importance of relationships in the process of learning and the development of a self. He pointed out that our self-concept is built through confirmation by significant others and shaped by the people we meet along the way, be they friends, teachers, authors of books, bosses, or mentors. He added one more relationship—our relationship with the spiritual, however we define it. The speaker presented a convincing case for the importance of relationships in shaping our identities and our concept of self. Moreover, he reminded those of us in the audience of the simple truth that all the knowledge in the world is worth nothing if it is not shared with others who care.

I remember thinking about the words of the wise leader for a long time after his presentation. It occurred to me that several people had influenced my self-concept and still were. But there was one more piece to the puzzle that didn't hit home with me until several years later. Just as the wise leader had predicted, this missing piece came from a relationship, in this case the relationship was with a professor. The missing piece was this: We need each other to *confirm* our self-worth. Let me try to explain what I mean by this.

In his controversial book *The Presentation of Self in Everyday Life,* Erving Goffman proposed that each of us presents a self daily to an audience, the most important member of which is ourselves (Goffman 1959). Indeed, one of the most important functions of language is to persuade ourselves and others that we are persons worthy of recognition. When we communicate with each other we seek confirmation of self. If we do not get it, or in other words, if we perceive that others, especially others whose opinions count such as our parents or our bosses, do not think much of us, we are devastated. Our self concept, our pride in self, is temporarily destroyed.

Environments in which people confirm each other are full of a special power. It is a power that emerges from people who feel good about themselves and receive energy from connecting to others. It is a power that the people who care for their work and each other know from firsthand experience. On the other side of the coin, environments in which people are encouraged to look out for themselves or taught to be selective about who they care for stifle the human spirit. In the short run, these environments can produce results, but over the long haul they suffer from a lack of community spirit. They are deprived of the power of relationships. Indeed, they often suffer as a result of negative energy that draws people's attention, thus their energy, away from their work and each other.

Caring Relationships Make Work More Enjoyable

Now, to my fourth and final point: cultivating caring relationships at work is fun. Dutch historian Johann Huizinga proposed the provocative thesis that all social institutions start as games (Huizinga 1970). In other words, someone did it the first time just for the fun of it. It is only later when the game turns into serious business that the fun disappears. In the case of the military complex, the game can even become deadly. One can speculate that the game of economics and business started as a game that was fun to play. People experienced pleasure doing it. Unfortunately, as the industrial era proved, the game of business turned into serious business. Driven by our need to make more things faster, we created complex systems that were controlled by huge organizations. Eventually these organizations defined work for us. In the process work lost its natural element of fun. In some cases, the game of business turned into a viciously competitive game. Intoxicated by the game itself, we threw ourselves into the battle and ignored the consequences to our relationships.

Mihaly Csikszentmihalyi discovered from his research with people who found joy in their life that fun is a by-product of engaging in meaningful work (Csikszentmihalyi 1993). This finding is a far cry from what most of us were led to believe by a culture that reinforced the notion that work must be drudgery and that leisure time was the time for fun. Work was thought to be a necessary evil that was enjoyable now and then if you were lucky enough to get the "cushy" job. Not so, wrote Csikszentmihalyi. We experience fun when we define a goal that matches our capabilities, develop the skills to achieve it, make a game out of it, share it with others who care, and actually lose ourselves in the game.

Huizinga's thesis that institutionalized activities started as fun becomes a reality when we observe work groups who are busy caring for their work and each other and having fun doing both at the same time. They show us that when we tap into our natural inclination to work together and have fun doing it, we actually improve the quality of our relationships and our work. Fun is a powerful source of energy. People who experience fun in their work report having accomplished far more than they thought they ever would. They discover that working, having fun, and caring for each other is contagious. When we experience it, we naturally want to experience it again.

Summary

If caring makes so much sense, generates a power of its own that is contagious, and is just plain fun, why don't we care for each other more often? The answer to that question is as deep as the roots of our evolutionary beginnings. For as we know only too well from our own experiences, even though cooperation makes good sense and we are programmed to work together and care for each other, we are also programmed to compete and inclined to elevate our self-image, even if, at times, that means we compete at the expense of others.

In truth, we have been bringing out the darker, win-lose competitive side of our relationships in the organizations in which we work for a long time. We have been driving caring relationships underground and pretending that we are nothing more than sharks, predators and parasites who look out for themselves and seek to grow at the expense of others. One of the consequences of driving caring relationships underground was to accent our fear of each other. The less we practiced caring, the greater our fears became. One of the lessons to be learned from the field of psychology is that the best way to deal with our fears is to embrace them, recognize them for what they are, and consequently deprive our fears of their source of energy: our attention. Our fears live off the energy we give them by either dwelling on them or denying their existence. By focusing on them we become our fears. On the other hand, when we confront our fears and actually embrace them, they lose their power over us if for no other reason because we see them for what they really are. In turn, we are released to care for others. The fear that keeps us from getting close to each other is no different. Therefore, we must embrace our fear of each other so that we can be free to care for each other. First, we must understand our fears, which is the subject of the next chapter.

6

Embracing Our Fear of Each Other

> But if we are able to see our own shadow and can bear
> knowing about it, then a small part of the problem
> has already been solved.
>
> . . . CARL JUNG

Relationships are a mixed bag for most of us. If your childhood was anything like mine, you grew up with good and bad experiences, starting in the most sacred institution of them all—the family. Perhaps you watched your parents fight, or worse, felt the tension of a cold war, the kind of tension that can be cut with a knife. Many people watched relationships fall apart and end in divorce. Some were victims of physical or verbal abuse from those who were supposed to love them and give them their very sense of self, a number that is higher than we would like to admit.

It has been said that we all come from dysfunctional families, it's only a matter of degree. After all, parents are not perfect. This being true, it is unrealistic to expect them to raise children without some scars from the process. In more relationship-centered cultures, the extended family made up of relatives and community members picks up some of the slack. If one failed to be confirmed as a special person in the family, chances are a caring relative or friend would make up for it. In some cases, special groups at work helped someone find a significant role in a group of people who cared. But the extended family, once a touted hallmark of life in the United States, was not a part of many people's experience in the mobile 1970s and 1980s. Even groups at work fell apart as a result of layoffs or were turned into cross-functional teams whose members changed monthly, if not more often. Relationships were further complicated by confusion over issues of sexual harassment and diversity. People no longer knew where the boundaries lay and what was acceptable behavior toward others. Teachers and managers were afraid to get too close to people they cared about for fear that they would say or do the wrong thing.

At the same time that relationships were changing, we were being encouraged to be strong, autonomous individuals in need of no one. Bellah and his associates discovered that the heroes of the industrial era were cowboys and detectives, fix-it specialists who rode into town, made everything okay, and then rode out again (Bellah et al. 1985). It can be said that the detectives are still with us. We call them *consultants*.

In a society based on strong individuals, to lose control of your emotions is to show weakness. We save emotions for our romantic relationships. Robert Solomon, author of a book on the subject of love, made the provocative observation that because we avoid relationships and love in the community and at work, we pour all our emotions into romantic relationships, creating false expectations and overburdening a relationship that is not equipped to handle it (Solomon 1990). In other words, we set ourselves up for failure because we create a false picture of what romantic relationships are all about. We expect them to magically appear as we fall in love and to sustain themselves without effort while we go about our life and work. Furthermore, we hold all our emotions in check at work and pour them out at the doors of our homes. No wonder marriages are overburdened. No single relationship can handle the full load of our emotions.

Solomon made another observation that is critical to our understanding of our fear of each other and to our fear of relationships. He pointed out that we relate to others and create a "love world" with someone or a group of others in part to form an identity—to create a self. In years gone by and in some cultures today, the extended family and the community shaped one's identity in the context of a group. Today in Western cultures the romantic relationship is burdened with the entire load of creating a shared self and an identity. Partly because the family, the church, the community, and the workplace—once social structures that supported identities—are in disarray.

Nowhere has the ethic of the strong, autonomous individual permeated our thoughts and actions more than it has in the workplace. Indeed, many of our managers and executives were promoted on the basis of their ability to hide their emotions, especially the emotion of love. In the workplace we were encouraged to "put our feelings aside" and make rational decisions, as if our rational thinking could be separated from our emotions, a fact that is convincingly disputed by scientists who have studied the human brain. Antonio Damasio reviewed several case studies of patients with brain damage and revealed that when people lose the ability to translate gut feelings into emotions (to merge the body and the mind), they also lose the ability to plan and to make rational decisions (Damasio 1994). New discoveries are being made about the mind-body connection and the role of emotions in what is often perceived as rational behavior. The truth is, it is impossible to separate the heart from the head just as it is impossible to separate relationships from work. Even if we could separate them, it is doubtful that it would be good for us or our work.

The point I am trying to make is that our experiences with relationships are likely to be a mixed bag. What's more, the bag is probably full of some stuff that is not very pleasant. Thus it is natural for us to fear close relationships. To add to our fears, we are not very practiced at the art of caring for each other. We have been encouraged to hide our emotions, especially at work. As a result, we are afraid to get too close to each other for fear we will do something wrong.

There are several reasons we are afraid to get too close to each other. I have compiled a list to help us get our arms around some of our fears. It is not my list alone. It includes the insights of those who have studied intimate relationships for years and borrows much from experts in interpersonal and small group communications. The list is not intended to be complete; it is intended to be a start to which you can add from your own experience. It is designed to stimulate dialogue, not to provide all the answers.

Fear of the Unknown

The first fear on the list is the fear of the unknown. Perhaps it is first because its roots are lodged deep in our evolution and our anxiety over fate and death itself.

Earlier I suggested that we are programmed to care for each other. It is also true that we are programmed to be suspicious of that which we do not know and understand. And for good reason. Early in our development we learned that the pussycat could turn out to be a saber-toothed tiger or that the friendly tribe in the village down the way could turn into a hostile group of intruders. One could argue that eventually, our fear of the unknown became a self-fulfilling prophecy. We learned only too well to be suspicious of each other, and we developed elaborate weapons to protect ourselves from each other. What's worse, we decided that the best way to eliminate the threat of invasion was to eliminate the potential intruders. Unfortunately, the tribe in the neighboring village possessed a bomb that was capable of blowing up both us and them.

In spite of the progress we have made in understanding our fears, we are still programmed to be cautious around strangers. Frankly, when we do not know or understand each other it pays to be cautious. Evolutionary psychologists further remind us that being cautious was likely a survival tactic that worked quite well for us when the only people we were likely to meet that we did not know personally were from neighboring, sometimes hostile, tribes. In other words, our genes are coded to make us suspicious of strangers, and rightly so.

In a world where people are disconnected from each other, everyone becomes a stranger. For all we know, the person who is driving the car next to us might be carrying a gun and be intent on using it. To complicate this matter, at times it seems as if the news media would like us to believe that everyone is potentially out to get us. We are dished out one disaster after another on the evening news. To bring this back to a benign, everyday level, in the workplace we are taught to be careful of those with whom we work for fear that they will use us or step on us on their way to the top. Our fear of physical harm from the unknown has been replaced with the real threat of losing our jobs.

The threat of harm implied in the fear of the unknown is a real one. In a way, it is born out of fear itself. Anthropologist Ernest Becker suggests that we are programmed, if not biologically at least socially, to seek revenge and put down our enemies, thus eliminating the possibility they will ever put us down (Becker 1975). Indeed, we equate justice with revenge. We believe that somehow we will be able to eliminate our fear of each other if we eliminate our enemies. What once served us well, a healthy cautiousness around strangers, has turned into a fear of others that has led to distrust and violence.

As Mihaly Csikszentmihalyi points out, to compete for scarce resources is natural to the human species, as it is to all species. Unfortunately, some leaders inside the organization have taken this to mean that it is natural to compete with each other. Harvey Mackay reminds his readers that we are all descended from sharks. Thus, win-lose competitive behavior is both natural and justified (Mackay 1990). Indeed, he points to progress as a natural product of our competitive nature and suggests that competing with each other is good for progress.

Just because our genes are coded to help us survive, and yes, compete for scarce resources, does not mean that we must "win" at the expense of our environment and the other creatures with whom we share it, including other people. On the contrary, as Mihaly Csikszentmihalyi reminded us, the best way to compete over the long term is to cooperate (Csikszentmihalyi 1993). Unless we learn how to cooperate in our use of limited resources, like the dinosaurs that preceded us, we won't be around to win anything. The challenge is to move beyond our fear of the unknown and discover common ground in the knowledge that the very fear we share is part of our being human together.

Fear of Fighting

The second fear on my list is the fear of fighting. I could have called it the fear of conflict, but I chose the word *fighting* for a reason. One reason is the term *conflict*, not unlike other popular terms of our time, has been complicated through overuse. I'm not at all certain we know what *conflict* means anymore. Another reason to call this the fear of fighting is that it is more to the point. In other words, what we really fear when differences are exposed is that a fight will break out and chaos will result. Or that some will win and others lose. Or that everyone will lose.

In their book about intimacy, poignantly entitled *Straight Talk*, Sherod Miller and his associates get right to the heart of conflict by declaring that when we say we fear conflict what we really mean is that we fear fighting. Furthermore, they maintain that the fear of fighting prevents people from learning how to talk openly with each other about differences which is a necessary prerequisite to dealing with conflict (Miller et al. 1982). They conclude by asserting that conflict can be healthy for everyone if handled in a way in which the individual is respected and everyone stands to gain new knowledge and insight about the issue and each other.

Unfortunately, too many of us grew up in families in which fighting meant putting others down, or worse, doing physical harm to each other. Or we grew up in families in which conflict was avoided at all costs. Sensitive issues were stuffed under the rug and never dealt with, resulting in repressed anger and heavy loads of guilt. As a consequence of not dealing with conflict, we grew to fear fighting.

Child psychologist Bruno Bettelheim reminds us that at the root of the fear of fighting is the assumption that if a fight breaks out chaos will ensue and someone will be hurt, or worse, they will leave (Bettelheim 1960). Usually it is the loss of a parent that is at the core of this fear. That's why people choose to stay in unhealthy situations. It's as if they say to themselves: "As bad as things are, at least I know what they are."

Unfortunately we all know people who seem to enjoy conflict, seizing it as an opportunity to put someone down as would a shark after a wounded dolphin. Perhaps it is the sharks who are the most afraid, but knowing that does not diminish the destructive power of their behavior. They only reinforce the fear that conflict will erupt into a win-lose fight.

There is another reason we fear fighting. It has to do with the rules of the game itself. By that I mean the basic assumptions that shape our thinking about the consequences of a disagreement. The basic assumption, or if you prefer a more popular phrase, the existing "paradigm," is that in a fight one party wins and the other loses or that if nothing is resolved, both parties lose. The loss we fear the most is loss of self-esteem. Indeed, sociologist Erving Goffman suggests that people fear losing face in front of people who count more than they fear physical harm (Goffman 1959). The higher one climbs the ladder of success, the more one's self is defined by status, power, and the trimmings of success, and the greater is the potential loss.

To embrace the fear of fighting we must be willing to challenge our assumptions and consider the possibility that both parties gain knowledge, understanding, and insight about the issue and each other when they listen to each other and deal with differences openly. That conflict need not end with winners and losers; differences can lead to new growth. This is a point I come back to in the chapters that follow.

Healthy dialogue, the kind that deals with issues and respects personal differences, the kind that honors the individual and keeps put-downs at a distance, is good for us. A dialogue over conflicting views, when it deals with the issues and respects the individual, can be a learning experience. Indeed, we grow through dealing with conflict openly. The worst thing we can do is to deny ourselves the learning process that takes place when we deal openly with conflict.

In truth, we can deny conflict and avoid fights, but that will not resolve anything. The issue will come up later, often in ways that hurt us and those we love. It behooves us to embrace our fear of fighting and to encourage open dialogue in the spirit of love and respect, even when it means learning through conflict.

Fear of Speaking Out

Another fear that keeps us at a distance from each other is the fear of speaking out. To speak out is to expose our ideas, our very selves to criticism. Like the fear of physical harm, its roots run deep, finding their way into our existential guilt for sticking out in creation. We equate losing face with an indictment for being frail and human. People who have experienced the embarrassment of looking stupid in front of their peers, or worse the boss, because of something they said often shy away from speaking out again. But the truth is, we all share in the fear of speaking out. Business author Chris Argyris noted that those who appear the most confident are more afraid of saying something wrong or stupid than the rest of us (Argyris 1993). That is why they repeat clichés and aphorisms they know are accepted by the audience and therefore won't get them into any trouble. In other words, they say only what they know the audience wants to hear.

Like the fear of fighting, the fear of speaking out also has roots that extend into the fear of loss of self and relationships. By speaking out one not only risks looking stupid and losing face but also risks losing the respect and love of people whose opinions count. Speaking out also can result in conflict and fighting. Thus it is connected to the fear of fighting.

Ernest Becker suggested that humans share a common predicament: our heads stick out in the midst of creation (Becker 1975), and we don't know quite how to deal with this predicament. Often we seek to hide in the crowd. If for no other reason, we feel safer in a crowd. We can share our common predicament, or as Becker suggested, share our existential guilt for sticking out in the first place.

The fear of speaking out and asserting oneself, like other fears that haunt us, is frequently reinforced in the family or the community where we grew up. I am reminded of my own upbringing and the messages I received as a child to be humble, which I took to mean that I should put myself down. Over the years, I have learned that false humility, the kind that encourages me to refrain from speaking out or put myself down, is not good for me or the people who love me. Nonetheless, the issue is still very real, and others I know are dealing with similar messages that they received as children.

Healthy work environments send messages to their members that each person is special, that speaking out, when done in a way that respects others, is very healthful. In fact, it is unhealthful not to speak out. Contrary to what we have been told, keeping our place is not good for us, for others, or for the learning that takes place when ideas and views are shared. At the same time, we must recognize that each person speaks out in his or her own voice. For example, someone who is introverted speaks out after much reflection, whereas those of us who are more extroverted prefer to think out loud from the beginning.

Becker was right. Our heads do stick out in creation. We are blessed with self-awareness and given the responsibilities that go with it. We should be proud of our calling and carry out our responsibilities with our heads held high. In the profound words of South African President Nelson Mandela, "there is nothing enlightened about shrinking so that other people won't feel insecure around you." Speaking out from our own inner strength and reaching out to others with love is what builds caring relationships.

Fear of Claims and Responsibilities

One of the lessons to be learned from those who study interpersonal communication is that the more we get to know each other, the more we open ourselves to claims that are implied in the relationship itself (Bormann 1990). To be a friend to someone is to be willing to accept his or her peculiarities and to demonstrate a willingness to stay in the friendship even when things become messy—in other words, to be responsible to one another. It is not a relationship to be taken lightly. That is why to enter a friendship is to take a big, often frightening step.

In the industrial era we learned how to avoid the claims and responsibilities inherent in close relationships by hiding behind the organization. One might say that the organization became an invisible shield to hide behind when we wanted to avoid caring relationships and the claims that go with them. The all-too-common phrase, "it is for the good of the organization" was used to excuse managers from taking responsibility for making decisions that affected people and relationships. Another technique used to avoid caring relationships was to call people issues the "soft stuff." The very words themselves suggest that the issue is not worthy of a busy executive's time. In reality, the reason we called people issues the soft stuff was that they were really the hard stuff. By calling it soft, we excused ourselves from the claims and responsibilities of venturing closer to people in order to get at the source of an issue. Once again, we ran away from caring relationships at work.

When we dare to approach each other and get to know each other at deeper, more intimate levels, we open ourselves to claims and responsibilities, but we also open ourselves to the joy that is ours only if we share common ground and build caring relationships with each other. What's more, we discover new dimensions of ourselves in the process. The claims found in caring relationships become the joys of sharing a life and task in common.

Fear of Being Disappointed

To enter into a close relationship is to risk being let down, disappointed by the behavior of those who are supposed to care for us. Like most of our fears, the fear of being let down can become real in early childhood experiences.

Perhaps a relationship with a parent, sibling, or significant other did not live up to its expectations and we felt the pain and disappointment of being let down. Or maybe someone threatened to abandon us by what that person said or how that person acted when we needed him or her. Even if our childhood experiences were

good ones for the most part, the fear of being disappointed can become very real, partly because the expectations set by the culture
that we live in are not real. The illusion that people live "happily
ever after" just because they love each other has been reinforced for
years and has provided unrealistic pictures of what relationships
are all about.

More recently, relationships have been receiving new attention.
Authors are writing books about energy fields that magically appear
when we let go of our illusions or when we trust in the self-organizing principles of the universe. No doubt these messages are a welcome relief to the messages of the autonomous individual who was
in need of no one, but we must be careful lest we set up unrealistic
expectations of what building caring relationships is all about. The
truth is, building caring relationships is more like learning to dance.
Sometimes the rhythm carries us across the floor; at other times we
just can't seem to get it together. The old aphorism that relationships
require hard work is true, but so is the truth that relationships need
to be nurtured with fantasy. To live in a love world is to live in a
fantasy that is made real.

Two other factors in the thinking of the industrial era contributed to unrealistic expectations regarding relationships. One was
the false picture of the autonomous individual, who, we were led
to believe, needed no one. The other unrealistic picture was painted
with broadcast and print media—the mass media—by those hungry
for our attention and therefore willing to feed us images whether
they were real or not. Often these pictures were paradoxical, some
even contradicted each other. On one hand, those who worked in
the mass media appealed to our nostalgic yearning for better times
with pictures of happy families and involved communities; on the
other, we were lured into modes of pessimism by pictures of violence and chaos. No doubt, users of mass media had learned well
how to tap into our aspirations as well as our fears.

In his book on love, Robert Solomon offered insight into the
romantic relationship in Western cultures that can help us understand our fear of being disappointed by our relationships. Solomon
revealed the history of romantic love and showed how the relation-

ship itself grew to be idealized complete with cultural myths about "falling in love" and "living happily ever after" (Solomon 1990). According to Solomon, the idealization of romantic love can happen only in a culture in which the individual is valued more than the group. Why? Because the self is only a self in relation to other selves. In a society in which relationships are hard to come by, it's hard to discover a self. Let me explain further.

Once the individual is freed from the constraints of the family, the clan, the group, and the community, he or she loses an identity (a self) that was tied to a role within the group. The individual must then go out and discover his or her "self." Solomon suggests that this is accomplished through romantic relationships with a significant other. In other words, we form romantic relationships in order to discover a self. In a culture in which other relationships no longer exist, romantic relationships are one of the few ways to form connections. This issue is especially poignant for men in our society who were expected to be rugged and autonomous. Romantic relationships in Solomon's view carry a large portion of the burden for defining the self. Indeed, Solomon suggests that the very reason we engage in romantic relationships is to discover a self.

In the 1950s and 1960s the myth of the "happily-ever-after" romantic relationship extended to include the family. Popular television shows like "Leave It to Beaver" and "Father Knows Best" complemented the romantic relationships already institutionalized by Hollywood and offered us yet another false picture of what it means to live in harmony. People grew up expecting to find happiness and fulfillment in romance followed by children and a perfect family. Reality, however, was not at all what we saw on the screen. Behind the scenes, broken relationships and abuse in the family were rising. These events ironically were turned into sensational stories in the same media that exploited the myth of the romantic relationship and the happy family in the first place.

In a society in which the individual is set apart from the group, romantic relationships and family are not the only place where one can choose to define a self. The other place where the self is shaped is at work. Prolific business author and lecturer Warren Bennis made this point clear in a speech I heard not long ago with his famous understatement, "work really defines who you are." Apparently, this is a truth that was not considered when decisions were made to down-size organizations. Indeed, if the illusion that the organization would take care of its loyal members was ever thought to be real, the reality has been shattered by the layoffs and reorganizations of the 1990s. The myth of the "happy family" at work has been destroyed once and for all by the realities of our time.

Movements to revitalize the spirit of community at work are gaining momentum. Etzioni's *communitarianism* movement is but one example (Etzioni 1993). In the workplace cross-functional teams are the rage. Respected authors like Charles Handy are calling for communities at work (Handy 1994). But people are cautious—and rightly so. Even when teamwork has taken hold, it has often been translated into a pattern of running from team to team while trying to keep up with a heavier workload. Unfortunately, a relatively small number of consultants who teach teamwork truly understand the dynamics of relationships within work groups or appreciate the truth that relationships permeate everything we think and do. In truth, there is no such thing as purely a task issue.

Given what has transpired over the past few years, it is no wonder that people are cautious of relationships. We only need to be let down so many times before we began to doubt the rhetoric of relationships and trust. The truth is, we will let each other down again. Relationships are not perfect. They are full of conflict. They require a conscious effort, a willingness to be responsible and to care for one another, and an ability to create new myths and fantasies in full knowledge of reality. They are also the only way we will continue to develop as whole, healthy persons. If we are going to persuade people, ourselves included, that relationships are real and that we mean what we say when we talk about trust, we will have to show it with our actions. People are waiting to see if the leaders in the community and at work really mean it when they tout meaningful relationships as being important and call for trust. Only then will we embrace our fear of being let down and move on.

Fear of Loss of Self

In Western cultures the self is a very real thing. Indeed, as the great sociologist of the self Erving Goffman pointed out, the self is sacred. We are willing to protect it with our very lives. Furthermore, we like to think of the self as a force, a spark, an inner flame with an indivisible integrity. It is often defined as an entity unto its "self," as if the self exists without relationships. From what we know now, however, the self is shaped by our experiences and our relationships. As Csikszentmihalyi puts it in his book on the evolution of the self, "the self is more in the nature of a figment of the imagination, something we create to account for the multiplicity of impressions, emotions, thoughts, and feelings that the brain records in consciousness (Csikszentmihalyi 1993, p. 216). We are what we pay attention to.

The self is a fairly recent invention in the overall scheme of things. Not that long ago, self talk was thought to be a conversation with the forces of the cosmos or a god. The idea of a self separate from tribe and kin was unheard of, or at least novel, as recently as 3,500 to 4,000 years ago. However, in the agricultural era and even more so in the industrial era, the self took on a life of its own. People eventually came to believe that the self was a little person inside of them that controlled input and output, a fixed entity with which one was born and kept unchanged throughout life. Csikszentmihalyi uses the analogy of a traffic police officer who directs input on the basis of previous and current experiences and relationships to describe the self (Csikszentmihalyi 1993). It is shaped continually by that to which we pay attention and that to which we fail to pay attention. Consequently, one who focuses all his or her attention on work or the organization and neglects relationships at home or at work becomes the work or the organization. For years, the common term used to describe someone who gave all his attention to the organization was the *organizational man*. In the past few decades, the organizational man was joined by the organizational woman. Lately, both are questioning why they gave their all to an entity that does not give back—at least the kinds of rewards that are lasting.

The self is a very sacred thing indeed. We fear the loss of self as much as we fear death itself. This is the thesis Pulitzer prize–winning author Ernest Becker put forth in his iconoclastic book, *The Denial of Death* (Becker 1973). Even more shocking is Becker's revelation that in Western industrialized cultures, this need to protect our "selves" has trickled down to impressing each other at work. To use Becker's words:

> It is only in modern society that the mutual imparting of self-importance has trickled down to the simple maneuvering of face-work; there is hardly any way to get a sense of value except from the boss, the company dinner, or the random social encounters in the elevator or on the way to the executive toilet. (p. 15)

Becker's poignant words remind us that our sense of self is related to our sense of control and consequently to our sense of power over a given situation. That is why relationships that ask us to be vulnerable and expose our selves can be frightening, especially for those whose self is built on a title or a certain social status.

George Herbert Mead and the sociologists of everyday life from the University of Chicago shed more light on the concept of the self (Mead 1967). They proposed that the self develops through stages that involve taking the role of the other. Even when we think we are alone we still carry the input of others whose opinions are waiting to emerge as our memories reconstruct them in our heads. Mead called these people in our heads the *generalized other*.

Because we are defined by our relationships, every time we relate to someone or something we risk being changed. We are particularly vulnerable to being changed when we disclose parts of ourselves or allow ourselves to be open to new inputs and diverse cultural views, which is why relationships are so very frightening. Our very self is at stake.

If we protect ourselves from each other we may be safe for a while, but we do not grow. The self is enriched through relationships. We become more complex selves in the process of relating to others.

The great Carl Jung compared people who have engaged in deep and meaningful relationships to gems that develop many facets. A self with many facets is open to shining in many ways. It is a self made stronger by and through its relationships to a history, a place, nature, a meaningful purposes, and most important, caring relationships with others.

Summary

In the past several pages I have presented six fears that keep us from getting close to each other. These fears are fueled inside the modern organization by the paradigm of the strong individual and the emphasis on growth and profits at all costs. For years we have rewarded independence, the ability to make decisions on one's own, and the presentation of strong, autonomous selves. To love and care for each other at more than a surface level was to risk appearing weak and touchy-feely. However, the opposite is true, if the self is made stronger by and through its relationships. We have been developing weak selves by emphasizing individualism at the expense of relationships. We traded our connections with nature, significant others, meaningful purposes, and the people with whom we work for connections to things in the form of symbols of success, lifestyles, and the organization itself.

Child psychologist and survivor of the Holocaust Bruno Bettelheim commented frequently on the good and bad aspects of Western cultures (Bettelheim 1960). Like Carl Jung and others, Bettelheim asserted that a strong self is built through strong connections to others. But he went a step farther. Bettelheim maintained that a major concern in a society based on autonomous, independent selves is that the self is weakened to the point that it becomes vulnerable to the control of the state and big organizations. In other words, strong relationships are needed to mediate the relationships between the organization and the people. All the more reason we must embrace our fears of each other and find ways to connect and build strong relationships that respect individual differences. Perhaps the workplace can play a leadership role in making this happen.

There is another reason we avoid getting too close to each other at work. Simply put, we aren't very good at it. Why? Because we haven't been practicing. We are afraid that we will botch it up. An analogy for this point is a broken limb. If you have broken your leg or arm and worn a cast for several weeks you know what it is like to lose the use of your muscles. Without regular exercise the muscles lose their tone, strength, and agility. The term for this is *atrophy*. So it is with the loving, caring muscles of the heart. If we don't use them every day, they atrophy. The only way to bring strength back is to exercise the muscles of the heart by loving and caring for each other.

Practicing the art of building healthy, caring relationships is not an easy undertaking. Our fear of intimate relationships and the responsibilities and claims that go with them will continue to hold us back. But there is hope. As I suggested earlier, caring relationships at work did not go away—they went underground for a while. People continued to practice the art of loving and caring for each other even in the midst of the shadows cast by the big organizations created in the industrial era.

We can bring caring relationships out into the open where they belong. However, it will take a conscious commitment to holding a life and task in common and a willingness to embrace our fears—to trust that through the process of building relationships our very selves will be made richer. We must become convinced that we can indeed move from *I* to *we* without losing *me*.

7

From I *to* We *Without* Losing Me

Who is the "I" separate from the "we" who has the hubris to
think that it acts in isolation?

> . . . JOAN BORYSENKO *Fire in the Soul*

Just as we have learned to separate ourselves from each other
and from the environment, we now need to learn how to
reunite ourselves with other entities around us without losing
our hard-won individuality.

> . . . MIHALY CSIKSZENTMIHALYI
> *Flow: The Psychology of Optimal Experience*

Perhaps it is time to pause in our journey and acknowledge the
other side of this issue. After all, intimate relationships and strong
ties to a clan or a group can restrict the growth of the individual.
Indeed, freeing the individual from the constraints of tribalism and
unhealthy relationships is one of the great accomplishments of Western societies. In the past two centuries alone slavery has been exposed for the evil it is, abusive relationships have been brought out
into the open. Women, children, and minorities have been afforded

the opportunity to crawl out from dependent relationships and express themselves in new ways. Granted, we have a long way to go with these issues, but we have made progress. In this century alone the United States achieved new heights in affluence and offered more people opportunities to take part in our achievements. Shouldn't we have the right to be proud of our accomplishments? And are we not wise to be cautious of the restrictions of relationships?

There is a shadow side to our accomplishments. For one thing, not everyone was able to participate in the affluence we created. In his controversial book, *The End of Work*, Jeremy Rifkin pointed out that there have been losers as well as winners in the game of success (Rifkin 1995). In fact, millions of laborers and middle managers have been displaced by technology. An unfair portion of these are minorities. Rifkin warned us that if we do not take notice of these trends and find ways to engage more people in meaningful work, we will create a permanent underclass that will be forced to find its own way to survive in the system. Unfortunately, inequities of opportunity are not the only issue. Our relationships to our work and each other have been damaged by our overemphasis on individual achievement and success.

To be human is to be connected. Spiritual writer Frederick Buechner said it plainly: "You can survive on your own. You can grow on your own. You can even prevail on your own. But you cannot become human on your own" (Buechner 1991, p. 46). To neglect our relationships for the sake of personal achievement or out of fear is to risk losing our humanity. There are those who would take this a step farther and suggest that our very self-concept depends on relationships.

Bruno Bettelheim reminded us that societies that offer the individual multiple ways to succeed require strong citizens capable of making wise choices and sharing the wealth with those who are not able to succeed by the rules of the game (Bettelheim 1960). To put it into Bettelheim's befitting metaphor, a society that offers rich food and unlimited possibilities to succeed requires people with strong stomachs, strong minds, and caring hearts. I think what Bettelheim was trying to tell us is that when a society offers its members multiple ways to succeed and an overwhelming number of "things" to pay attention to, people need strong selves able to discern between alternatives and make wise choices.

Here is the irony. If strong selves are built through strong relationships, how does a society help its members build strong selves without robbing people of the freedom to express themselves in unique ways and to "become persons" to use the words of Carl Rogers (Rogers 1961)? How do we move from *I* to *we* without losing *me*? This is a difficult question that deserves more than a terse answer. Perhaps the place to start is with the concept of freedom itself. Maybe being free is not really freedom. Let me explain this paradoxical statement.

Freedom as we have come to understand it has its price. While freeing the self to achieve success, we set ourselves apart and made ourselves vulnerable to another kind of control—control by the system itself. Anthropologist Edward Hall reminded us that when the self is released from the ties and constraints of the primary group, such as the family, the tribe, or the clan, or the work group for that matter, our ties and constraints are transferred to our creations (Hall 1976). People created systems in order to expand their natural drives and abilities, like the drive to learn and to work. In the United States and other Western countries, work translated to producing goods and services "efficiently and effectively" for the sake of progress. To paraphrase the words of a popular slogan of the 1950s, "Progress is our most important product."

Hall revealed that the systems we created in order to become more "productive and efficient" took on a life of their own. They became extensions of our natural drive. The organization became an extension of our natural drive to create and to work. In the same manner, our school systems became extensions of our natural drive to learn. The systems we created required our complete attention and loyalty as a source of energy. But here is the catch. Eventually, the system takes over the natural human drive. Hall called this phenomenon *extension transference*. In other words, we transferred our natural drives to learn and to work to our institutions and organizations. Eventually the systems defined learning and work for us, including why we should work with stimulus-response, reward-based theories of motivation; how and with whom we should work, with its elaborate command-control structures; and when we should work, with time-clocked schedules and ritualized meetings. As a consequence, we were no longer in control of our work or our learning. The system was in control.

How do we free ourselves from the control of the very systems we created without giving up the value of social structures. Anthropologist Dorothy Lee suggested that part of the problem integrating personal freedoms with social responsibilities in the West lies in our definition of the concept of freedom. We define it as *freedom from* as opposed to *freedom to* (Lee 1987). We often talk of freedom in the context of *have to.* "I don't have to work on Sunday," we say, "therefore I am free to do whatever I want." Yet, Csikszentmihalyi's research revealed that Sunday is the least happy day of the week for many people (Csikszentmihalyi 1990). Bettelheim called this phenomenon "Sunday neurosis" and describe it as boredom and frustration over nothing to do mixed with anxiety over having to return to the drudgery of work on Monday (Bettelheim 1960). Csikszentmihalyi's research ironically showed that people were the happiest when they are at work (Csikszentmihalyi 1990). In other words, happiness is a by-product of working at something one loves to do in the presence of people who care.

The separation of freedom from responsibility in Western cultures prompted psychologist and author Viktor Frankl to assert that what is needed in the United States is a statue of responsibility on the west coast to complement the Statue of Liberty on the east (Frankl 1984). But a statue by itself will not solve the dilemma. We still must find ways to integrate the self back into the group without losing the hard-won freedoms we have gained.

Part of the answer to our dilemma lies in our past. Eastern philosophies and religions promoted the capability to integrate the individual into the group and the flow of the Universe itself without losing the respect for each unique person. It is embedded in the concept of *harmony*, which Csikszentmihalyi defined as the capability to *differentiate* and *integrate*. He writes:

> Differentiation refers to the degree to which a system (i.e., an organ such as the brain, or an individual, a family, a corporation, a culture, or humanity as a whole) is composed of parts that differ in structure or function from one another. Integration refers to the extent to which the different parts communicate and enhance one another's goals. (Csikszentmihalyi 1993, p. 156)

A society that promotes harmony honors the individual as both a unique person and a part of the group. A society or an organization that is only differentiated (promotes only individual achievement) risks becoming chaotic and disconnected. One that promotes only integration will be smothering. Harmony (or *complexity* as it is called in the new sciences) involves the optimal development of both differentiation and integration.

Dorothy Lee's work provides examples for our edification. The book contains some of the more profound insights about the self and society ever written (Lee 1987). Lee's insights emerged from having spent several years living in cultures in which groups of people seemed to have mastered the art of living in harmony. To put this in simple terms, they had learned how to move from *I* to *we* without losing *me*.

For Lee, freedom and responsibility are connected. In truth, to be free is to be free to be responsible to nature and others. What's more, intimate relationships need not deprive the person of an identity; rather, caring relationships provide a source of energy and actually strengthen the self. The individual in a society that practices harmony (promotes both differentiation and integration) is twice blessed, once as a unique person and again as a valued member of a special group.

The cultures studied by Lee differ from each other in many ways, but they have one characteristic in common: a strong value and respect for human dignity, what Lee calls the "sheer personal being" of each individual. And it is not subject to compromise. An example from her book helps explain this point.

Writing about the Navajos, Lee points out that respect for the individual is at the core of their beliefs and forms the fabric of their social structure. In fact, respect for the individual is so important that no one is allowed to speak for or make decisions for another person. This includes the children. To speak for someone, would be "fundamentally indecent." Even leaders are not given permission to speak for or to make decisions for others. Authority is for clarification; it is not a position of command and control. One consults the leader much as one would the dictionary or the knowledge of an Einstein. What's more, individuals never humble themselves in the presence of the leader or anyone else. To do so would be to insult the gods who created them.

The insights of Dorothy Lee and others who have studied societies that have mastered the art of living in harmony offer much to help us understand the modern-day relationship between the self and the organization. When we lose respect for the individual and consider people to be human resources that are expendable, we give ourselves permission to treat each other as if we are only objects—human resources. We do damage to our relationships. In the process we lose the fabric of our social structure: our relationships with each other. We are forced to hold things together with rules, regulations, and plans administered and policed by managers. Lee is quick to remind her readers that societies in which people live in harmony are not free of structure. In her own words, "Unstructured freedom, whether fenced or not, is still namby-pamby" (Lee 1987, p. 57). But structure is shaped and held together with caring relationships that build trust. It has the characteristics of a skeleton, in contrast to boxes, the cubicles and private offices we have constructed in the modern organization. Groups are held together by common bonds of friendship, shared visions, values, and goals.

Creating the kind of work communities where people care for their work and each other is not easy. It takes a group of people who consciously commit to holding a life and a task in common. Work takes on a whole new meaning. It is an expression of the self, but it is also connected to the group and the community at large. That is why Lee calls the experience of working in caring groups being twice blessed: once as a special person capable of a significant contribution, and a second time as a significant member of a special group (Lee 1987).

Western cultures have adapted a distorted view of the self and society. A false dichotomy exists that pits the individual against society. We fear being sucked in by the crowd and the loss of our freedoms. Ironically, we are some of the best conformers in the world. We dress alike, talk alike, drive the same cars, and live in houses that look alike.

Perhaps we can learn about strong selves from cultures like those Dorothy Lee studied. Not so we can copy them, for that is not possible. Even if it were possible, we would soon discover the same human shortcomings that are with us today. But we can still learn truths from them like the truth that there is no self without an other. The self develops in relation to significant others and continues to be shaped by relationships throughout life. This does not mean that we must give up our individuality. On the contrary, our special and unique skills and perspectives blend with our experiences and relationships to shape the special persons we are continuously becoming. In truth, it is our very differences that give our relationships meaning and depth. Anthropologist Gregory Bateson suggested that we come to know and truly love ourselves and each other through our differences (Bateson 1979). As the philosopher and theologian Martin Buber put it, "a person…realizes his uniqueness precisely through his relation to other (different) selves" (Friedman 1965). What's more, when we share our unique selves with other selves we become even more special and unique by adding new dimensions to ourselves. To repeat the metaphor introduced earlier by Carl Jung, deep relationships shape facets of ourselves that shine when the light hits them so that we appear as radiant jewels. The more deep relationships we have, the more facets we have and the more opportunities we have to shine like diamonds.

When we build relationships with each other based on an unconditional respect for the individual and trust in each other, we move from being individuals to being part of a greater whole without losing our unique identities. We go from *I* to *we* without losing *me*. In a world in which technology is reinventing the way we interact with each other, it is important that we do not lose sight of this truth. We would be wise to learn from societies that have mastered the art of living in harmony to differentiate the self, develop complex selves with many facets, and respect diversity while integrating our unique selves into work groups, organizations, and societies that promote harmony with nature, each other, and the forces of life itself.

Moving from *I* to *we* without losing *me* is not easy. It requires embracing the shadows to challenge our basic assumptions about our work life and our relationships. A change of this magnitude asks us to lose the self to gain the self. When confronted with a change of this magnitude, we need to engage our hearts and our hands as well as our heads. The digital language of words, logic, and quantified results is not enough. We must appeal to the older, more perfected analogical language found in stories, myths, and metaphors. In the next section of the book I return to a metaphor introduced in the story that began this book: gardening. But before returning to the garden, let me share two stories about relationships at work.

He who bends to himself a joy
Doth the wing'ed life destroy;
But he who kisses the joy as it flies
Lives in Eternity's sunrise.
                    . . . ROBERT BLAKE *The Joy Is in the Dance*

A good relationship has a pattern like a dance . . . .
                    . . . ANNE MORROW LINDBERGH *Gift from the Sea*

Several years ago, while traveling as a marketing manager for a major food company, I found myself with some extra time on my hands in a hotel that faced the beautiful beaches of Carpenteria, California. The buyer of a major customer I was to have visited that afternoon had canceled our appointment. It was an unusually warm day in March. Fully aware that weather like this was at least two months away in Minnesota, I decided to take advantage of it and strolled down to the beach.

On the beach a group of children were busy building sand castles. They were some of the most elaborate structures I had ever seen, complete with turrets and drawbridges made out of sticks. As the construction projects took shape, the children moved from moments of intense work to spurts of laughter and celebration.

When a castle was completed to the satisfaction of their own inspection, the children danced around their creation holding hands in a circle, laughing and falling down on top of each other. But as things go, the joy of the moment was destined to be interrupted.

Two of the boys broke from the dance. They stood in front of the castle with arms folded, jaws set, and eyes squinting in a mean stare. For some reason these boys had decided that the castle belonged to them and that they must guard it from the others. The others were quick to pick up the challenge and began to taunt the guards. They knew the script well. One of the intruders kicked sand in the general direction of the prized castle, just close enough to cause a reaction from the guards. The others joined in with a few well-placed kicks of their own that spread sand just inches from one of the castle's turrets. The game of tease and retreat continued for several minutes. Eventually two of the children tired of the game and moved to a new location, where they began to construct another masterpiece. Others followed. Abandoned by the intruders, the boys who had chosen to guard the castle began to fidget. With no intruders to fight off, the life of a guard was not much fun. Before long all the children were lost in the art of castle building once again.

Watching the children build sand castles reminded me of a truth I had lost sight of over the years. It is a truth that children seem to know intuitively. The truth is this: the joy is in the dance.

As our egos develop, and we take on social customs (in other words as we "grow up"), we forget that working together can and should be fun. If it isn't, it loses something. Or as chief executive officer and well-known business author James Autry put it, "If it doesn't, then we're wasting far too much of our lives on it" (Autry 1991, p. 13). If we fail to pay attention, the older we grow, the better we become at protecting our castles. We make the mistake of defining ourselves by the size and value of our castles. We grow to believe we *are* our castles. And like the boys who decided to guard the sand castle on the beach, we stand guard over our status, lifestyles, and possessions ready to defend them against any and all intruders. Unfortunately, unlike the boys on the beach, adults never tire of guarding ourselves and our possessions. We have a hard time letting go long enough to join the dance.

Working together around a life and a task in common can be magic, as the children building sand castles on the beach discovered. Anne Morrow Lindbergh captured this magic in the metaphor of the dance. Every now and then I run into a work group that has discovered the joy of the dance. They laugh a lot. Sometimes they fight. And like the children on the beach, sometimes they get tangled up in protecting their own castles. But they always seem to be able to get back into the joy of their work together. They often appear lost in the sheer joy of their work. Like the children, they have learned that the joy is in the dance itself.

But let's face it. Getting along with people at work is not as easy as building sand castles with a group of friends. Charles Conrad, who wrote several books on organizational communication, called relationships at work "unnatural" to make the point that we seldom choose the people with whom we want to work (Conrad 1985). We frequently find ourselves thrown into a group and forced to get along or else. Sometimes it works and sometimes it does not.

In spite of the "unnaturalness" of relationships at work, now and then we run into a group of people who really seem to care for their work and each other. Like the children building sand castles on the beach, the members of the group have discovered that the joy is in the dance. You know when you are in such a group by the way the work flows naturally around caring relationships. People often describe the experience as the best group they ever worked with. If you are lucky, you have been part of a special group like that at least once in your work life. I have been lucky enough to experience a group like this more than once, but one in particular holds a special place in my heart.

There was something special about our group. Perhaps it was captured in the words of our theme for 1988: We Care. The idea behind the theme was to promote the message that we cared for our products, our customers, and each other and that as a result we would continue to grow and be profitable. At the time, not everyone bought into the theme, but most of them agreed to go along with it anyway. I suspected that those outside our division, especially those in upper management, wondered whether we had gone too far with this "caring stuff." I know they wondered why we were having so much fun in our work. The message to stick to business had been delivered more than once. But no one could argue with our success. In fact, we contributed more profits per employee than any other division in the company.

A comment from an old friend who recently reflected with me about the Division That Cared over a cup of coffee brought clarity to my own thoughts about the experience. "We didn't realize what we had," he said. My friend was right. Too often, we fail to appreciate what we have until we no longer have it. For my own part, it was only in retrospect that I learned to fully appreciate the sense of belonging that permeated the group in spite of (or perhaps because of) the normal human conflict that we struggled through as we learned to relate to our work and each other.

The Division That Cared wasn't perfect. Life is not like that. We experienced the normal conflict that emerges when egos bump and world views clash. Sometimes we handled these differences well in the spirit of open dialogue and learning. Other times, we blew it completely. Some people left the group as a result of hurt feelings or unrealized dreams. But we grew through it all.

When we reflect on our experiences, it's always easier to remember the good times. For example, I remember the creative sessions with the marketing department trying to come up with a magazine ad that would properly promote whey—a by-product of cheese making that was less than glamorous, to say the least. It was an impossible task. But that didn't stop the agency from trying. I can still see the sour look on the face of the marketing manager when the ad agency presented us with: "How do I love thee? Let me count the wheys." If I am not mistaken, that very ad won an award that year. But I also remember the conflict between production and marketing and how we failed to learn from it because we were too busy stuffing it, pretending everything was just fine. How easy it is to forget the bad times.

The most important thing I remember about the Division That Cared is the tolerance and respect for each other that grew as we learned to know and care for each other at a deeper level. I especially remember the people who were there for me when I felt down and depressed or when I was physically ill with cancer. Whether we intended to or not, we began to care for each other at a deep level.

Sometimes I ask myself how a group of misfits within a large organization grew to care for each other and still outperform expectations. I don't have a good answer to that question. But I think part of the answer lies in the relationships themselves. Like the children I watched building sand castles on the beach, we lost ourselves in the rhythm of our work and our relationships with each other. We discovered that the joy is indeed in the rhythm of the dance.

I am no longer a part of the Division That Cared, though a part of me will always be with them. Much has happened since then, including layoffs and reorganizations. But they seem to have weathered the storm with a minimum loss of people, and the spirit of caring still seems to be alive. I do know that those who are still there continue to produce results that are admired by management. From what I can observe at a distance, it has something to do with the fact that they still care for their work, their customers, and each other. And that they have not forgotten that the joy is in the dance.

III

Cultivating Common Ground: A Process for Building Community at Work

Developing the capacity to cultivate a shared form of life may make the difference between a personal life rich in connection and meaning and one bereft of lasting satisfaction.

...ROBERT N. BELLAH, RICHARD MADSEN,
WILLIAM M. SULLIVAN, ANN SWIDLER, STEVEN M. TIPTON
The Good Society

8

What's in a Metaphor?

And the Lord God planted a garden in Eden, in the east; and
there he put the man whom he had formed.

. . . Oxford Annotated Bible, Genesis 2:8

Asking what's in a metaphor is like asking what's in a picture, a
story, or a feeling. You have to close your eyes and use your senses
and your imagination to get at the answer. You must see the picture
the metaphor creates in your head, hear the sounds it produces,
smell the scent of the images it presents, and touch them with the
fingers of your mind. That's what makes metaphors so rich. To use
the words of a professor I once knew, "metaphors are laced with
truths unencumbered by facts."

I chose gardening as a metaphor to bring out the truths about
relationships at work. Because it seems to me that caring relationships at work are a by-product of working together around a shared
task. To borrow the words of a dear friend, community is about making a conscious commitment to holding a life and a task in common.
And that's what gardening is all about.

The process of gardening itself is not unlike building healthy,
caring relationships. For one thing, gardening starts long before the

plants emerge from the soil. One must clear the ground and prepare the soil first—much like the process of clearing out old assumptions that keep us from building caring relationships at work. In the process of clearing out old assumptions, we discover common ground and begin to see beyond our fear of intimacy. Once the seeds for growth have been planted, we must be patient and wait for them to take root, trusting in the forces of nature to help the process along, not unlike the process of getting to know, care for, and trust each other. It helps to fertilize the ground just as we fertilize relationships with our work and each other with meaning and purpose. Months of cultivating and caring for their growth finally results in the harvest, but not without storms of conflict along the way. Relationships, like sturdy plants, grow stronger from weathering the storms of conflict. There is hard work in gardening, but there is also joy—just as there are hard work and joy in the building of relationships. Like the joy of building caring relationships, a big part of the joy is found in the work itself. The other part is in the joy of sharing our work with others.

I can also think of some practical reasons to use the gardening metaphor. For one thing, it is growing in popularity. More people are discovering the joy of gardening together as a way of building community. Gardening clubs are popping up in large cities and in small farming communities around the country. In some areas, the movement has even taken on a name of its own, such as the Community Supported Agricultural Movement in my own state of Minnesota. An Internet search for "gardening" reveals approximately 100,000 matches. Suffice it to say, gardening is a familiar metaphor that is regaining its popularity with a growing number of people.

It is not the practical reasons or its growing popularity that prompts me to use gardening as a metaphor. It is the pictures gardening conjures up in my head when I let my intuition and my heart do the work. It is then that I begin to see people cultivating the ground together, working with their hands, their heads, and their hearts while sharing in the joy of their work and their relationships with each other. I hear people laughing together and crying together, learning through their very differences and growing through conflict. I feel people being present for each other. I envision people working alone at times and at other times sharing in the work of the harvest. I sense the joy of the dance.

Something happens when people make a conscious commitment to holding a life and a task in common. They discover the magic of the dance. What's more, they discover what it means to belong to a group of people who will be there for each other when the time comes. They come to know that there is power in caring relationships.

If caring relationships emerge in the new organizations of the twenty-first century, it won't happen as a response to an edict from above. It will happen because ordinary people like you and me made a conscious commitment to plant and grow gardens in the workplace, to hold a life and a task in common. With that thought in mind, I invite you to join me as I further develop the metaphor of gardening. I hope to capture what it really means to make a conscious commitment to holding a life and a task in common. Most of all, I hope the metaphor of gardening conjures up pictures for you of people working together with their hands, heads, and hearts, caring for each other, releasing the power of relationships at work.

9

Clearing Out Old Assumptions

> Good relationships and personal connections can come only when you abandon the patterned thinking and language of business.
>
> ... JAMES A. AUTRY
> *Love and Profit: The Art of Caring Leadership*

Every gardener knows that before you plant the seeds you must plow the ground. Before you can plow the ground you must clear it of old shrubs, rocks, and other foreign material that can inhibit the growth of the plants. So it is with building community in the workplace. Old assumptions about relationships at work must be cleared before new, healthier relationships can emerge.

I have compiled a list of assumptions that I believe must be cleared at the ground level before we can release the power of relationships at work. The list is by no means complete. Indeed, I hope to add to it as I learn more. But it's a start.

Assumption One
Assemble the best people, and you will create the best organization.

Although we don't always come out and actually say it, there is an implied assumption in many organizations that the way to create the best "winning" organization is to hire people who work and think alike. Some organizations even test potential employees to make certain they fit a preferred profile. This assumption comes to life when we recruit the top students from the "right" colleges or when we eliminate people who do not fit the mold. In small group research this assumption is called the *assembly effect* (Bormann 1990).

Research to prove the assembly effect has shown mixed results. In fact, the Minnesota Studies conducted by Bormann and associates suggest that groups of high performers have a difficult time working together (Bormann 1990). For one thing, they all want to be the leader. Susan Cohen's study of a corporate restructuring team that ended in conflict and indecision is a good example of what can happen when several strong leaders are suddenly thrown into a team (Hackman 1990). Groups of the best people occasionally click, but it often has more to do with the clarity of the task, the emergence of healthy social and task norms, and the ability of the group to help each member discover a meaningful role than it has to do with the specific talents of specific individuals.

In their book, *The Knowledge-Creating Company: How Japanese Companies Create the Dynamics of Innovation*, Takeuchi and Nonaka (1996) point out the importance of middle management, which seems to go against the trend in the United States, where the role of middle managers has been downplayed. According to Takeuchi and Nonaka, teams of people who are close to the products and the customers promote innovation and learning. In an interview published in the April 29, 1996, issue of *Fortune* Takeuchi elaborated on this point and added, "Japanese companies rely on innovations from groups of ordinary people. They depend on middle managers' trying to push everyone on the team up to a higher level of shared understanding." In other words, it is relationships in groups of ordinary people that stimulate innovation.

Summarizing several case studies of work groups in real organizational settings, Richard Hackman (1991) identified "points of leverage" that enhance group task performance. Under group structure, Hackman found group composition to be a factor. The research showed that whereas the group needed the right skills for the task, it was more important that the group learn how to function well as a group. More relevant to the point, Hackman found that diversity can lead to new learning, whereas a group of all the best has little to learn from each other.

The research seems to say that assembling the right people is a small part of building an effective community at work. Good practices and processes along with healthy relationships between members have more to do with it. I would challenge the assumption that to create the best team you need the best people. Productive teams are like healthy, productive communities in that they are made up of ordinary people doing extraordinary things together.

Assumption Two

If I become part of a community, I will lose my identity.

I won't spend too much time challenging the assumption that we lose our identities when we become part of a caring community at work. I deal with the move from *I* to *we* in chapter 7. It might serve us, however, to revisit a couple of points.

The fear of losing the self is particularly poignant in low-context cultures, in which individual freedoms are seen as "freedoms from" and valued above the needs of the group (Hall 1976). But as Dorothy Lee's work (1987) suggests, individuals are strengthened by their relationships to the whole. In other words, we don't have to give up our unique identities when we become part of a caring community at work. Indeed, in a group of people who care for their work and each other the self is twice blessed, as an individual and as a valued member of the group. Maurice Friedman quotes the philosopher and theologian Martin Buber: "It is from one (person) to another that the heavenly bread of self-being is passed" (Friedman 1965, p. 71).

Species that learn to live in harmony, in other words, to differentiate the unique gifts of each person and to integrate those gifts for the benefit of society, find joy and meaning in their work. In truth, the evolution of the species as well as the growth pattern of the individual is a process of differentiating and integrating that contributes to the rhythm of life.

Theory and philosophy aside, the fear of losing the self in the crowd is real in the workplace. I know more than one chief executive officer (CEO) who truly believe with all their hearts that if they dare to be intimate with their subordinates, they will lose their personal strength, their very sense of identity. To use the words of one CEO, "I will lose control."

Perhaps it is this sense of control that is at the heart of the matter. In fact, one could argue that our very identities are based on our sense of control. To lose control is to lose "self," a thought that leads to the next assumption that has to be cleared away.

Assumption Three

If I get too close to people, I will lose control.

"Whatever you do, don't let yourself get too close to your people." These words of advice were addressed to me by my boss when I was promoted to my first supervisory position in customer service in the late 1960s. I suspect I'm not the only one who heard these words. They were rather common in the 1950s and 1960s. They can still be heard in the organizations of the 1990s.

To understand our fear of losing control, it might help to retrace the origins of our command and control structures themselves. The anthropologist Edward Hall offers help (Hall 1976). He reminded us that in low-context cultures in which individual freedoms are valued above ties to the group and freedom is defined as a freedom from, the rules for holding things together must be administered from the outside, because the more intrinsic controls found in high-context cultures are absent. Whereas in high-context cultures people avoid certain behaviors because they are afraid to disappoint someone or because they fear the shunning of the group, in low-context cultures one is free to do what one wants to do. Dorothy Lee likens the structure in high-context cultures to a skeleton in that the social structure is held together from the inside by caring relationships (Lee 1987). Command and control structures, on the other hand, are more like fences or boxes that keep people in line.

There has been a recent call for self-managed groups. Popular books like *Leadership and the New Science* by Margaret Wheatley tell of structures held together by relationships (Wheatley 1994). Charles Handy wrote about the need for even more trust between people in an era when command and control structures can no longer keep up with the need for learning and information (Handy 1994). Perhaps we are being forced to learn that we do not lose control when we dare to become close to others. We might learn that controls built from caring relationships are much stronger than those administered from a distance. The richness of the gardening metaphor lies in its power to take us beyond our fear of losing control. In the process of clearing the ground of false assumptions, we will discover that to lose control is to gain control of our work and our relationships.

Assumption Four

If I let my emotions out, I won't be able to make rational decisions.

This assumption is closely connected to the assumption that caring relationships will lead to a loss of control. In this case, however, the fear has more to do with the myth of rational behavior. In reality, the hierarchical, command-control structures of the organizations of the industrial era were based on the belief that people are rational. For the most part, we still believe that.

To start the process of clearing the ground of this false assumption, I refer to the work of Antonio Damasio (1994). In his book aptly titled *Descartes' Error: Emotion, Reason, and the Human Brain,* Damasio destroyed the illusion that the mind and the body are disconnected. He provided several real-life examples to make his point. Citing work with patients who suffered damage to certain parts of the brain believed to control emotions, Damasio revealed that without the ability to connect our feelings to our rational processes, we cannot plan effectively. The work is far too complex to describe in a few short sentences, but the following quotation from the book begins to capture what Damasio is trying to show us.

> The apparatus of rationality, traditionally presumed to be *neo*cortical, does not seem to work without that of biological regulation, traditionally presumed to be *sub*cortical. Nature appears to have built the apparatus of rationality not just on top of the apparatus of biological regulation, but also *from* it and *with* it. The mechanisms for behavior beyond drives and instincts use, I believe, both the upstairs and the downstairs: the neocortex becomes engaged *along with* the older brain core, and rationality results from their concerted activity. (p. 128)

I think what Damasio is trying to tell us is that the head, the heart, and the gut are connected. In other words, it is impossible to behave rationally without our emotions. We can't even when we try.

When I look for real-life examples to validate Damasio's discoveries, I am quickly and wonderfully rewarded. All that I need to do is reflect on the times when I was part of a greater cause that I felt in my heart and my gut or when I was part of a group of people who truly cared for their work and each other.

We love to play both sides of this rational-emotional game. When it is time to please the boss or a discerning board of directors, we put on our best serious face and spout out numbers, market shares, and trends. Then when it comes to executing our plans, we call for loyalty, dedication, passion, and the "extra mile"—all the emotional stuff we are supposed to avoid.

If we are going to release the power of caring relationships at work, we must clear the ground of the assumption that our emotions will get in the way of rational decisions. Maybe the best way to do that is to engage our hearts and our hands in the process of clearing the soil together so that we operate with a clear and informed head and make our decisions with passion and compassion.

Assumption Five

By showing that I care for people, I will appear to be a weak leader.

This assumption has been around for years. It is firmly embedded in the social structure of corporate America. As Bellah and his associates reminded us, the cowboy and the detective became the heroes of the industrial era (1985). We were supposed to put on a face that showed we needed no one and were in complete control of our emotions at all times, including, or perhaps especially, in times of stress.

In an age of the enlightened manager, one might think that this assumption no longer holds water, that the cowboy has ridden off into the sunset and taken the detective with him. The truth is, however, that there are plenty of John Waynes still around. In fact, in the past six months I have heard dozens of managers bring out the old cliché "when the going gets tough, the tough get going." Or to put it into the language of the organization, as a manager did for me recently: "What we need around here are fewer people going to seminars and talking about sensitivity and spirituality and more people who are willing to do what is needed for the bottom line."

In a hypercompetitive world the cowboy and the detective are still around. In fact, statistics show that as a people we are working harder, longer, and under more stress than ever (Schor 1991). Many managers are afraid they will look weak or not competitive enough if they take time to care for people. Nonetheless, if we hope to build healthier relationships with our work and each other, we must clear the soil of this assumption, begin to cultivate common ground, and release the power of relationships at work.

Henri Nouwen wrote a profound little book called *The Wounded Healer* (Nouwen 1972) about the power of being vulnerable and caring for each other at a deep level. He suggested that we serve ourselves and each other best when we share our wounds. Therefore, the wounded healer, the one who dares to be vulnerable and gets close to her people, might just be the stronger leader. Janet Hagberg wrote a book with a similar theme, aptly titled *Real Power* (Hagberg 1994). She made the simple yet equally profound point that power is not power until you give it away. In other words, real power is about reflecting and caring as much as it is about daring to lead and to act. In the final analysis the two are really one.

The assumption that we must avoid caring for each other at work is near and dear to me. I have always been "too sensitive for my own good," as my father put it. In fact, my first boss in business noticed this same weakness in me. When he promoted me to a supervisory role in the late 1960s, he was quick to warn me: "You need to change your ways now that you are a supervisor. Don't be so sensitive to people's needs. Whatever you do, do not get too close to your people. You never know when you will have to fire one of them."

For several months after that warning I worked hard at being tough and unemotional. I kept my distance from the people who worked for me. I ate lunch with my own kind (other supervisors) and was careful not to socialize with the troops. Finally, one of the people from my department mustered up the nerve to approach me. She was a friend who had worked with me for three years. I still remind myself of her words when I start to act too much like an executive. "You know," she said, "you used to inspire us with your enthusiasm and caring ways. We always thought of you as our natural leader. Now that you are our appointed leader, we don't know who you are anymore."

The words from my friend were a poignant reminder to me of a wise truth about leadership. Leadership is about relationships. As I point out later, leadership is a communal concept whereby leaders and followers work together around a life and a task in common in the spirit of community. In truth, caring for each other makes us stronger leaders. We are our best selves when, as leaders, we care for each other at deeper levels. It is a truth that the garden brings out for us.

Assumption Six

Conflict is about winners and losers.

Some of the most pervasive and difficult problems we face as managers can be placed under the heading "Dealing with Conflict." Part of the reason for this is that we don't deal with it.

Some of us would rather avoid differences or smooth over conflict for fear a fight will break out or that conflict will make things "uneasy." Others actually seem to revel in conflict, diving into a situation of conflict like a shark after a wounded dolphin.

What is it about conflict that makes us want to punish it, avoid it, repress it, or revel in it? Like most complex issues, this one has multiple roots that lead in many directions. At the heart of the matter is the assumption that conflict will result in winners and losers.

Most of us grew up in a world where conflict led to winners and losers and everyone risked rejection or humiliation. In truth, in a world of winners and losers, everyone is a loser. At the least, everyone comes out having lost face. The winners look stupid for having insisted that they win; the losers are humiliated for having come out at the short end of the stick. By playing the win-lose game, we fall into the trap of being victims of the game itself. Ironically, our efforts to protect ourselves by out-bullying the bully, make us either a victim or a bully in our own right.

We can resort to running away from conflict or pretending it away. But these tactics have consequences that are more dysfunctional than the conflict itself. Avoiding or repressing conflict only puts it aside so that it can emerge in another time and place. The CEO who berates the vice president for a late report might be, in reality, getting back at her for another, unrelated incident. Perhaps the victim of the CEO's wrath disagreed with a decision he made or pricked his conscience by reminding him of the consequences of his decision in the lives of the people who work for the company.

The assumption that conflict will lead to winners and losers is alive and well in the workplace. It can be heard in the boardroom in discussions of strategies and tactics to put the competition out of business. It can be seen in the shoulder shrugs and the frowns of powerful executives when they seek to put down a colleague. As the great sociologist Erving Goffman reminded us, we are artists at protecting ourselves and putting each other down (Goffman 1959). If we want to bring out the power of relationships at work, we must first clear the soil of the assumption that conflict is about winners and losers. We must accept our common humanity, seek out differences, and look at conflict as a natural part of working together and as an opportunity for learning and growth.

Assumption Seven

There is no time for socializing at work.

The seventh assumption is rooted in the mechanistic view of the world that has been with us for almost three hundred years. Behind the assumption is the notion that work is serious, rational business and that the task will suffer or things will get out of control if people are allowed to socialize too much. To challenge this assumption, I return to the discoveries in anthropology then proceed to recent research on small work groups.

Edward Hall reminded us that play, including what we often call socializing, is as old as our beginnings as a species (Hall 1976). Several species exhibit behavior that can be defined as play. All you need to do to grasp this concept is to watch puppies wrestle on the ground or go to the zoo and see monkeys chase each other from tree to tree. The truth is, animals and humans learn through play. Unfortunately, this truth has been lost in the bureaucracy of most organizations.

Small group research has revealed another implicit truth about relationships at work. In every group there is a social-relationship dimension as well as a task dimension. In reality, the two are not separate. They are merely ways of looking at the same interaction from two different angles. If relationships between members of a group are "out of sorts," the task suffers as well. The reason is at least twofold: one, there are too many hidden agendas around unresolved conflict; two, people's energy is used up by issues that draw attention, thus energy, away from the task at hand. In the end, the task suffers because the group is literally out of synch. Groups I know that suffer from unresolved, or "stuffed," conflict engage in wheel spinning and never seem to reach a decision on the task.

Every group has a rhythm of its own. Healthy groups learn to blend the social dimension into the task. However, every group is different and must discover its own unique rhythm. The best way to tell whether you have discovered the rhythm that works for you is to trust your experiences and your feelings. You can feel it when things are going well, and you can feel it when they are not. I have heard members of a group that is out of synch refer to the level of tension being so real that it was "as if you could cut it with a knife." Paying attention to relationships is critical to maintaining a healthy, balanced rhythm. Inside the organization it is often referred to as the *morale* of the group. Regardless of what we choose to call it, denying the social dimension of a group under the assumption that the task will suffer does harm to the group and the task. It is another lesson we can take with us as we learn to cultivate common ground.

Summary

I have shared some assumptions about work that I believe prevent us from tapping into the power of relationships at work. I realize that sharing false assumptions about relationships at work is only a start. By giving you a list, I am merely pointing out what might get in the way of healthy relationships at work. If the process is to be complete, like the gardener who removes the rocks, shrubs, and debris before plowing, we must find a way to remove these false assumptions. What's more, like the gardener, we must remove them with our hands and our hearts, not just our heads. Otherwise, the roots of the problem will remain and the weeds of discontent will grow at the earliest opportunity.

I have discovered several ways to engage our hands and our hearts in the process of removing false assumptions about relationships at work. One of the ways is to first write them down on a piece of paper or a flip chart, then crumble them with your hands and physically throw them in a waste basket, one at a time. It helps to engage the heart if each member of the group shares his or her feelings with the rest of the group as the old assumption is tossed away. Another exercise that engages the hands and the heart as well as the head is to break into small groups. The need for small groups and the size of the groups depends on the size of the department, division, or organization that forms the work community. The ideal size of the group is five to seven members. Each member of the group is asked to make a list of assumptions that he or she feels prevent healthy, caring relationships from emerging at work. Each member shares his or her list with the other members of the group. The group then decides by means of a process of dialogue and elimination which assumptions are the most destructive to caring relationships at work. It is important to translate the assumption into actual behaviors. That way the group can articulate behavior it wishes to exhibit more and behavior it wishes to exhibit less.

Fortunately, others have dealt with the need for embracing the shadows of our assumptions about relationships at work and offer ways to engage people's hands, hearts, and minds in the process. Marvin Weisbord's book *Discovering Common Ground* is an excellent resource (Weisbord 1992). He shared what other groups have done from multiple disciplines. With a more scientific paradigm Margaret Wheatley (1994) and Chris Argyris (1993) write about breaking old patterns, scripts, and rituals and releasing the power of relationships. At the heart of Peter Senge's popular book on learning organizations is the removal of old assumptions that get in the way of healthy relationships (1994).

Most experts seem to agree on one thing: it is important to bring everyone who is part of the work community into the process so that each person takes ownership and finds a way to become *actively* engaged with his or her hands, head, and heart. Unless this happens, the problems will not go away. The group will continue to pretend that relationships are not important, or worse, the group will disparage relationships as the "touchy-feely" stuff. As a result, the task and the people will suffer. If there is one message with which I wish to leave you at this point in our efforts to prepare the soil for building healthy relationships at work, it is this: Find a way to engage everyone in the process, beginning with a clearing away of the old assumptions about relationships.

I am closing this chapter, but I am not closing the book on removing unhealthy assumptions about relationships at work. In the chapter that follows I will deal with one more unhealthy assumption that keeps the power of caring relationships underground. The assumption to which I refer is so pervasive that it deserves a chapter of its own.

10

From Swords to Plowshares

And they shall beat their swords into plowshares,
And their spears into pruning hooks . . .

> . . . *Oxford Annotated Bible, Isaiah 2:4*

There is one more assumption that must be cleared away before relationships can blossom at work. It is perhaps the most damaging assumption of them all and therefore the most difficult to remove.

The assumption has deep roots that reach into our evolutionary beginnings. Like other living things, we are programmed to perpetuate our own kind. This programming includes a mechanism for warning us when our survival is threatened. We learned to fear the dangerous and the unknown, and rightly so. After all, the pussy cat could turn out to be a saber-toothed tiger. The problem is, this natural fear of the unknown has gone beyond its original purpose. We have gone from spearing tigers to spearing each other. Presented in an oversimplified version, our story goes as follows.

Once there was a creature who, like all creatures, was programmed to survive and perpetuate its own kind. Included in this programming was a natural fear of the unknown. The creature grew in complexity and eventually gained knowledge. Unfortunately, along with knowledge came an awareness of its own condition, including the awareness that it would die one day. The creature could not accept this terrible fate. Therefore it used its newly found knowledge to create symbols of power that could transcend its mortality. These symbols took the form of religions, ideologies, and systems complete with heroes willing to protect these symbols and keep them alive and growing. The creature also built weapons to protect its symbols. The weapons became so powerful that eventually the creature was able to threaten its own survival as a species. No one dared pull the trigger (at least not yet) lest he or she destroy the race.

Along the way, this creature, now blessed with knowledge, took on a self. After all, it needed something to filter all the information coming from its systems and relationships, something that could produce a sense of control. Eventually, the self, like the symbols created earlier, took on a life of its own. Now, the creature had one more thing to protect: its very self.

So goes at least one version of the story of humankind. As we grew in complexity and self knowledge, our fears also grew more complex. Before long, we were waging wars to protect our symbols. We continued to construct more complex ideologies and religions to overcome our increased fear of death. We elevated our strong and our wise to hero status and offered them loyalty and obedience. We developed cultures and systems that included large organizations to increase our control over our environment. We developed lifestyles to protect our self images.

Unfortunately, the very systems we created to protect us and to give us control over natural drives and our environment took on a life of their own. As they grew in size and complexity, the systems demanded more and more of our attention and protection. We still wage wars to defend our ideologies, our cultural systems, and our national boundaries, even though these boundaries are harder and harder to define. Those in power still protect our organizations. All of us practice our self-protection rituals and put each other down in an effort to keep our identities intact. In other words, while we wage wars against countries and our competition at a national and organizational level, we play put-down and gotcha games at an interpersonal level.

How does this translate into real life in the organization? Not too many years ago the author of a popular book suggested a metaphor that captures life in the organization (Mackay 1996). The metaphor was one of the most ruthless predators of all time—the shark. One of the messages contained in Mackay's book was that because we are sharks, the best way to survive in business is to outshark the sharks. What is so frightening about this is so many people identified life in the organization with the behavior of sharks. I can only assume that millions of people tried to model their behavior to outshark the sharks.

As the great Erving Goffman revealed, part of the problem lies in our very selves. In his book aptly titled *The Presentation of Self in Everyday Life* Goffman (1959) pointed out that in a society based on the ethos of rugged individualism, the self takes on a sacred status. We become masters at the art of self presentation, all the while protecting ourselves from each other. Several years later, Harvard Professor Chris Argyris echoed this truth after a five-year study with an executive team. Observing the lack of organizational learning, Argyris (1993, p. 2) wrote: "This individual embarrassment or threat is what has led to the organizational embarrassment and threat that has resulted in limiting genuine organizational learning." In other words, it was the fear of loss of self-esteem that kept people from changing and thus limited organizational change. People were busy protecting themselves from embarrassment.

My own research inside the organization revealed the lengths to which we will go to protect ourselves. Over a period of six months I observed the self-protection rituals of a group of executives who used Goffman's ritual called *role distancing*. Role distancing is the practice of behaviors, both verbal and nonverbal, such as shoulder shrugs and rolling of eyes, to keep the self from being contaminated by the situation or being identified with someone who might make one look bad in the eyes of a peer group. In essence, one protects oneself from going down with the role. An example of role distancing occurred when an executive I was observing rolled his eyes when a group of his fellow executives caught sight of him eating lunch with some old friends. Later, the executive reported that the message he was sending to his fellow executives was that he was only with this group of lessers because he had no choice. In other words, he was distancing his "executive self" from the self that appeared to be connected to the group he was with because he did not want his fellow executives to associate him with the old gang.

Not surprising, I discovered that self-protection rituals were a part of everyday interaction. Also not surprising was the discovery that the higher up the hierarchical ladder of the organization one climbed, the better at the art of self-protection one became. This discovery was consistent with the findings of Argyris. Having lived inside the organization for thirty years, I was not surprised by this discovery.

We are experts at the art of protecting our "selves"–even when it means putting others down before they have a chance to embarrass us. During times of rapid change when things are up in the air and we are no longer certain of who we are or where we are going, we become even better at it. It is as if we revert back to our win-lose ways, pull out our swords and stand ready to defend ourselves with our lives. Just because we are programmed to protect ourselves does not mean that we must compete with each other in ways that result in winners and losers, or worse yet, put each other down just to protect ourselves. In other words, we don't have to be sharks or learn to outshark the sharks who power our organizations. Mihaly Csikszentmihalyi (1993, p. 21) offers an alternative to the win-lose view of the world without denying our competitive natures:

> Competition is the thread that runs through evolution. Life forms displace one another on the stage of history, depending on their success in taking energy from the environment and transforming it for their own purposes. But often species survive because they have found ways to improve their chances of survival through cooperation. Paradoxically, cooperation can be a very effective competitive tool.

Whether or not humans are competitive is not the issue. It is how we compete and what we compete for that counts. As Csikszentmihalyi pointed out, the best way to compete over the long haul is to cooperate. Unfortunately, we have perfected ways to compete that are not good for us or our species. Fortunately, we are also programmed to cooperate. We can accept our competitive nature, and we can even benefit from it as we learn how to cooperate in ways that increase our individual skills and our ability to care for each other.

The metaphor introduced in the title to this chapter captures the essence of what it means to cooperate as opposed to the win-lose–lose-lose games we play while protecting ourselves from each other. If we take the energy we exert to produce weapons and to protect our very selves and redirect that energy into discovering ways to cooperate, we will benefit as individuals and as a species. The gardening metaphor captures what it means to work side by side with our heads, our hands, and our hearts, to turn our swords into plowshares. We can still hone our individual skills through healthy competition, but we can do it in the spirit of community.

Robert Bellah and his associates describe community using three terms that reinforce the wisdom of Isaiah. The first term they use is *settlement*. They define *settlement* as the "willingness to cultivate the purpose of individual and common lives rather than be swept along in the fervor of exploitation" (Bellah et al. 1992, p. 275). *Settlement* implies staying together long enough to let caring relationships form around a life and a task in common. The second term is *cultivation*, defined as the process of turning over the ground and discovering common purposes and then working together with our hands and heads on shared tasks. The third term used by Bellah and associates is *generativity*. By this they mean the care that one generation gives to the next. As we cultivate common ground together, we must always be aware of the consequences of our work for future generations.

Moving from swords to plowshares, from protecting ourselves from each other to cooperating in the spirit of community, will take more than a recognition of our past dysfunctional behavior. Although embracing the shadows is a good first step, we must take the next step and remove them symbolically using our hands and our hearts as well as our heads, much as we did with the other assumptions that got in the way of caring relationships at work. The suggestions I offered at the end of chapter 9 apply here. The important thing is to involve everyone in the process. Once we acknowledge the harm we have done to our relationships in the past, embracing the shadows so to speak, we are free to begin to accept our common humanity and our common ground.

11

Discovering Common Ground

It's the everyday things that give life its stability and its framework.

> . . . SUE BENDER *Plain and Simple*

Something happens when people clear the ground of old assumptions about relationships at work. In the process, they discover common ground.

In a book titled *Discovering Common Ground*, Marvin Weisbord shared several process models from his work with groups of people from multiple organizational settings in government and business who came together to solve an issue or work on a task (Weisbord 1992). Although the process varies from setting to setting, it always involves a process of discovering common ground around trends, events, assumptions, and relationships. Weisbord described the facilitation of the process as follows:

> Should people open old wounds, fight old battles, or jump to problem-solving, we seek to have them acknowledge each other's reality

and remind them that the task is finding common ground and future aspirations. As we discover them, that is where we plant our action flags. When we work on common ground and common futures, we tap deep wells of creativity and commitment. (p. 6)

Taking it a step further, Weisbord references the work of social psychologist Solomon Asch, and posits four conditions for effective dialogue (Weisbord 1992):

1. All parties are "talking about the same world," requiring that people back up their generalizations with concrete examples.
2. All human beings have basic psychological similarities, as regards "laughing, loving, working, desiring, thinking, perceiving, etc."
3. As a result of 1 and 2, "the facts of one person's world become part of the other's" and they develop "a shared psychological field."
4. If conditions 1, 2, and 3 are met, people will experience their common dilemmas in the external demands, events, trends, developments that shape *all* [emphasis added] of their lives, and plan accordingly.

A process unfolds as people roll up their sleeves and begin to clear the ground of assumptions that can get in the way of caring relationships at work. This process unfolds in the context of *real* issues, demands, events, trends, and developments. In other words, people must have a reason to come together. Often that reason is in the form of a shared task such as gardening.

Too often we form groups or teams, appoint a leader, and jump right into the task without taking time to discover the reason for being a group in the first place or give the members of the group time to get to know each other. Typically when this happens, the group follows along without being fully engaged. A story from a manager of a customer service department of a large food company is revealing.

Like many companies these days this one was going through a reengineering process. Part of the process involved establishing cross-functional teams. The manager of the customer service department was asked to join one of the teams, whose task was to improve the order-filling process. The team was given the assignment by the vice president of sales in the form of a brief memo that simply stated that the group was to improve the process and eliminate errors in shipping. In the same memo, the customer service manager was assigned to lead the group.

At the first meeting it became obvious to the customer service manager that no one was all that excited about being part of the group. It wasn't because the group disagreed with the need to improve order accuracy. Indeed, two of the group's members from sales had been complaining about short shipments and inaccurate billings for some time. Rather, the concern of the group centered on the question of whether it took a team to deal with the issue. Sales thought the customer service department should just go ahead and fix the problem on their own. Everyone agreed that workloads were such that taking the time to meet as a team just added to the stress of their jobs.

The customer service manager attempted to quell the concerns of the group by diving right into the task. "As long as we're here, we might as well make the most of our time together" were the words he used.

According to the customer service manager, the group did just what he asked them to. They jumped right to the task. However, most of the efforts were performed by individuals outside the group setting. The customer service manager produced a report that implied an improvement in order accuracy. However, sales insisted that the company was still making too many shipping errors. When asked about their experiences as a group, the reply from the members of the group was unanimous: "What group?"

You might say that the group in the story was never a work group. Unfortunately, the example is all too familiar. Research bears it out. Richard Hackman's findings based on research with small work groups in several organizational settings revealed that when group members are not given the time to understand why they are a group in the first place, they seldom become an effective group

(Hackman 1991). Hackman made the simple point that a motivational task or reason for being is at the heart of what makes a group effective. Like Weisbord, Hackman asserted that the group must be given the opportunity to discover its purpose for themselves.

There is a myth floating around corporate America that leaders have visions, set clear goals, and then motivate people to follow them. No doubt leaders need to share their own visions and set clear goals. For example, if the vice president of sales in the story had taken the time to introduce the task properly and had shown some enthusiasm, it could have made a real difference in the attitude of the people who were part of the group. By sharing their own vision and articulating clear goals, leaders can set the stage and help the group become motivated. Furthermore, leaders can motivate others by their own example. But *how* this happens in real life is more like a process than a revelation from above delivered by a charismatic leader. People discover shared visions and goals in the process of working together around real issues and tasks with their hands, heads, and hearts. This is another lesson the gardening metaphor can teach us.

Studies of small groups, like those Bormann conducted at the University of Minnesota, show that in real life people join groups because they see a means to express themselves or to achieve a desired end (Bormann 1990). In other words, people gather around common means that lead to common ends, not the other way around. We decide that we want to become part of a group because it is a means to getting a degree, making a living, or expressing ourselves and our beliefs or because it is simply a fun group in which to be. For example, in the case of the order-processing issue in the story, had the task been presented properly, some of the people might have chosen to be part of the group out of concern for improving the process.

Once in the group, we are turned on, turned off, or not moved one way or the other. If all goes well, we discover common ground around a task or a shared goal out of which a shared vision emerges. If all does not go well, we discover that what we thought was a group in which we could become excited about the people and the task turns out to be a group of people with whom we don't have anything in common and may not even like and a task that fits neither our skills nor our interests. The leader of the group can greatly influence our group experiences and can by himself or herself turn off people with abrasive behavior or a lackadaisical attitude. However, whether we discover common ground is determined by the interaction within the group and the relationship between the people and the task.

How this actually happens in real life has been outlined by Ernest Bormann in his book on small work groups (Bormann 1990). He describes the process of moving from an aggregate of individuals to a work group with a life and a task in common as a process of *symbolic convergence*. The term captures both the symbolic and process-oriented nature of group interaction. Moreover, it captures the essence of what it means to become a caring community at work. According to Bormann, to become a community at work is to discover common ground around a life and a task in common. Eventually, the group begins to share common symbols that tell much about the life of the group. These shared symbols can be in the form of a "founding" event such as a common crisis, a shared concern, or a task that must be completed. The best way to discover the shared symbols of a group is to listen to their stories. As the group interacts, people take on roles, and the group agrees to accept behaviors (norms) for socializing, including dealing with conflict, as well as for working on the task. The group takes on a shared language for "insiders" and may even name a group mascot. The members of the group share fantasies, myths, and stories that describe the character of the group and say much about its mode of interaction.

Harvard Professor Robert Bales first asserted that the symbolic language of a group is the key to understanding what is going on inside a work group (Bales 1950). Bormann took this concept a step further and conducted extensive research on group story telling or what he called *group fantasies* (Bormann 1990). He discovered that groups tell stories complete with heroes and villains that really describe what is going on inside the group. Thus a group that repeats

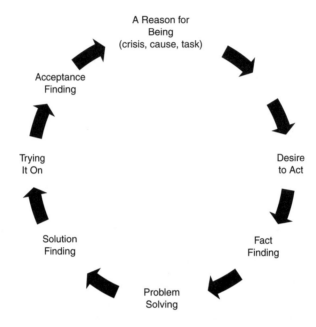

Figure 11–1   *The creative process.*

a story about the evil manager who laid off people without their input might be dealing with their own fear of being laid off.

I have attempted to capture the process of becoming an effective work group by modeling the creative process as shown in Figures 11–1 and 11–2. Figure 11–1 represents the creative process itself. It starts with a reason for being then moves to a desire to act, which leads to fact finding, problem solving, and playing with solutions (Remember: Humans learn through play). From there, the model moves to trying on solutions and acceptance finding, which takes the group back in a circular manner to the reason for being a group in the first place and encourages the group to renew their commitment to a task in common.

Figure 11–2 adds an inner ring to represent the inner life of the group. What this model attempts to show is that while working on a task, the members of a group discover common ground, deal with tension, discover meaningful roles, establish norms for acceptable

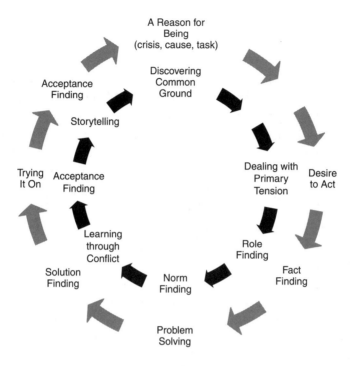

Figure 11–2   *The creative process expanded.*

behavior, learn through conflict, accept each other, and tell stories that reveal the workings of the group, and cultivate their relationships. It also shows that the task and relationship dimensions of the group are very connected. By connecting the two circles we began to capture what a community at work is really about. The outside circle captures the creative process while the inside circle addresses the social-relationship dimension of the group. In reality the task and relationship dimension are not separated, but for the purposes of understanding group dynamics, it helps to look at them side by side while remembering that one shapes the other.

I will return to this model throughout the chapters that follow. It is one way to show how groups discover common ground while working together with their hands, heads, and hearts around shared reasons for being while developing relationships with the task and each other. From the model it would appear that the process moves smoothly from one step to another. In reality, the process is sporadic and interrupted. The process itself is more like a story with chapters that surprise the reader with new plots and changing characters. The sporadic and often conflict-ridden nature of the process becomes clearer in the chapter on conflict (see chapter 15).

Releasing the power of relationships at work is about discovering common ground around our common humanity and a shared reason for being together. That's why gardening makes such an appropriate metaphor. Community is about making a conscious commitment to holding a life and a task in common. The commitment starts with a reason for being a community in the first place. Too often we expect people to form groups or teams without giving them a good, clear reason for doing so and a chance to discover common ground. The results are aborted team efforts that leave a bad taste in the mouths of group members and a hesitancy to get involved in teams in the future. On the other hand, groups that spend time discovering common ground begin to thrive and, like gardeners who get lost in the task of gardening, the members discover meaning and purpose in their work.

12

Fertilized with Meaning

> For the meaning of life differs from man to man, from day
> to day and from hour to hour. What matters, therefore, is not
> the meaning of life in general but rather the specific meaning
> of a person's life at a given moment.
>
> . . . VIKTOR FRANKL   Man's Search for Meaning

The concept of *meaning* is a popular topic these days. One could say that the concept of *meaning* has taken on new meaning. People wonder about the meaning of their lives, their relationships, their work, and the flow of life itself. Like other popular concepts of our time, the concept of meaning risks losing something through overuse. If I may continue with my play on words, the concept of meaning is losing its meaning.

Overuse or not, meaning is important. It is the fertilizer that helps the seeds of community grow. Rather than abandon the term altogether, perhaps we simply need to understand it better and put it into context. Let me start this process by sharing perspectives from two experts.

No one has written more about meaning than the renowned psychiatrist Viktor Frankl. In his book *Man's Search for Meaning*

Frankl shared his personal experiences as a prisoner and asserted his belief that meaning, or the lack of it, is the critical issue of our time (Frankl 1984). It is unfair to Frankl to summarize his insights in one short paragraph, but I will try to offer a "meaningful" summary that is relevant to caring relationships.

Frankl looked at meaning as the central focus of life. He suggested that one discovers meaning in three different ways: (1) by creating a work or doing a deed, (2) by experiencing something or encountering someone, and (3) by the attitude one takes toward unavoidable suffering. Frankl elaborates on the two aspects of the second point by referring to the example of experiencing nature or culture to clarify what it means to "experience something." "Encountering someone" is best described by referring to Frankl's own words: "last but not least, by experiencing another human being, in his [or her] very uniqueness–by loving [someone]" (Frankl 1984, p. 134). For Frankl meaning also has to do with suffering with dignity, because life, if we embrace others and live it to its fullest, is about suffering now and then. In the case of unavoidable suffering, meaning is discovered when one sees beyond the event or circumstances beyond one's control and finds meaning even when it is not obvious. Frankl captured this third way of discovering meaning by writing, "in some way, suffering ceases to be suffering at the moment it finds meaning, such as the meaning of a sacrifice" (Frankl 1984, p. 135).

Mihaly Csikszentmihalyi offered a definition of meaning in his book *Flow: The Psychology of Optimal Experience* that is similar to Frankl's definition, but has a different slant (Csikszentmihalyi 1993). Csikszentmihalyi's definition includes three dimensions. The first dimension is *purpose*. Meaning as purpose is the most common way to define meaning in Western cultures. When we say that our life lacks meaning we are, in essence, saying that our life has no purpose. We believe that our lives should strive to achieve a goal or complete a task, that our life should serve some purpose, that we should have a reason for being. If our life lacks purpose or if we can't figure out what that purpose is, we say our life lacks meaning. This dimension of meaning compares with Frankl's reference to discovering meaning in a work or a deed.

Csikszentmihalyi calls the second dimension of meaning *resolve*. This dimension is captured in the phrase: *I mean to do well*. In other words, I resolve to do something about my purpose in life. This usage dimension of meaning begs an interesting observation in Western life and thought. We judge people on whether they *meant* to do something or whether what they did was merely an accident. To mean to do something is to do it on purpose. This dimension takes meaning beyond merely having a purpose for life in one's head and requires that one show by intentions, and ultimately actions, that one intends to achieve that purpose. In other words, it is not enough to have a purpose, one must consistently resolve to do something about it. This dimension of meaning might be closer to Frankl's second way of discovering meaning in an encounter with someone or by experiencing something.

The third dimension of meaning involves the overall ordering of information or events. To say, "a red sky in the evening means fair whether tomorrow" is to give meaning to an event by connecting it to specific consequences, thus giving it an order. Csikszentmihalyi calls this third dimension of meaning *harmony*. This dimension connects with Frankl's third way for discovering meaning even in unavoidable suffering. One discovers harmony in one's life when what one does in the everyday connects beyond its everydayness to a life theme or a universal pattern. For Csikszentmihalyi, this requires differentiating oneself by expressing a special talent or skill and then integrating that talent or skill into the whole of one's life, the community, and ultimately, the Universe. For Frankl, this truth includes finding meaning in even the unavoidable suffering in life.

If there is a central theme to the meaning of meaning, it is found in the concept of relationships. Meaning is discovered in our relationships with ourselves, our work, each other, and the universe we live in. Meaning is discovered when we begin to cultivate common ground in the spirit of community. When we work together around a common life and task, we find meaning in our work (Frankl's task or deed), in our relationships with each other and our common experiences with nature and culture (Frankl's encounter and experience), and in our learning through conflict and suffering together (Frankl's meaning in unavoidable suffering). In the process of holding a life and a task in common we discover meaning in life and we come to know the true meaning of living in harmony with ourselves and each other.

The people I talked with about relationships at work while I was writing this book told me stories about departments and work groups that made them feel special and gave their work meaning. It was always in the context of a shared task and relationships with people who cared for their work and the people with whom they worked. I recall talking to Ann, who worked for a customer service department in a large insurance company. She and the rest of her department made it a point to help each other work in a high-stress environment. They created what they called time-outs whereby people could share their frustrations with others and just "be there" for each other.

Another example was a team of nurses on a surgical recovery ward who found ways to deal with multiple pressures from doctors, patients, and management by initiating a mentor program that involved people from all disciplines. At first it was difficult to persuade the doctors that they had time to participate, but those who found time actually reported that the time they spent mentoring released some of the stress in their jobs. As one nurse put it after reading Csikszentmihalyi's definition of meaning, "we had plenty of purpose and resolve in our work caring for patients, but we lacked the harmony created by healthy relationships with each other."

At this point it might help to bring back the model introduced in chapter 11 (Figure 12–1).

In the outer circle that represents the creative process, you will note that for a group to come together the members must feel a compelling reason for doing so. In other words, their coming together must be given meaning through a shared *purpose*. To do something about this shared purpose, the group must have a strong desire to act, a *resolve* to move into fact finding, problem solving, and solution finding. As the model shows, however, the inner life of the group must also grow and bring *harmony* to the group as the members discover common ground, deal with tension, define roles and behavioral norms, and cultivate their relationships and deal openly with conflict.

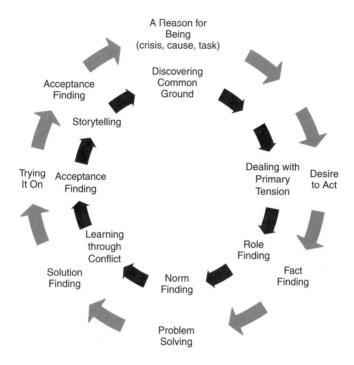

Figure 12–1 *The creative process expanded.*

Frankl is correct when he tells us that work without meaning is empty work. As Matthew Fox put it recently in a book about meaning at work, work without meaning is more like "being worked" or merely having "a job" (Fox 1994). Meaning and relationships are very much connected. In reality, meaning is discovered when we work together around a life and a task in common. There is no other way to find it. When we do discover meaning in our relationship at work, our lives take on a new depth and richness they did not have before. Meaning in the context of purpose, resolve, and harmony, acts like a fertilizer. It makes the ground we share more fertile. It enables growth of the seeds of our relationships and helps the seeds blossom in ways we would have never imagined.

13

Sowing Seeds and Nurturing Relationships

Oh the comfort the inexpressible comfort of feeling safe with a person; having neither to weigh thoughts nor measure words but to pour them all out, just as it is, chaff and grain together, knowing that a faithful hand will take and sift them, keeping what is worth keeping, and then, with the breath of kindness blow the rest away.

... GEORGE ELIOT

There are red letter days in our lives when we meet people who thrill us like a fine poem, people whose handshake is a brimful of unspoken sympathy and whose sweet, rich natures impart to our eager, impatient spirits a wonderful restfulness. . . . Perhaps we never saw them before and they may never cross our life's path again; but the influence of their calm, mellow natures is a libation poured upon our discontent, and we feel its healing touch as the ocean feels the mountain stream freshening its brine.

... HELEN KELLER

W̲hen I was a child, I loved to garden with my brothers and sisters, especially my sister Sandra. The part I loved best was planting the seeds. There was something about the act of putting a seed into the ground with my hands while Sandra packed the dirt behind me that made me feel part of life itself. As I pressed the seed with my thumb I would imagine it growing into a vegetable, and I felt as if I were part of the growth process itself. Not understanding how it worked, but not needing to. It was awesome enough just to be a part of it.

Sowing seeds as a child was one of those simple experiences that turned out to be a profound lesson for my life. For me, planting seeds is about building relationships—relationships with nature and the soil, with others who plant with us, with our work, and with deeper parts of ourselves.

Later in life, I discovered that working together was a lot like planting seeds with my brothers and sisters. Working together is about building relationships. If our relationships at work are out of sorts, our work suffers. Let me explain what I mean by this with another story.

After dropping out of college in the mid 1960s I took a job on an assembly line. I wasn't expecting much. I just needed some money to keep me going while I pondered a new major. I remember my first day as if it were yesterday. As one might expect, I was apprehensive about how I would be received. Much to my surprise and delight, things went better than I expected. The reason had to do with one special person.

I arrived early that first day, just to make sure I would not get off to a bad start. The personnel person who hired me was there waiting as promised. He hurried me into an orientation session, where I met five other nervous people like me. I was relieved to find company, and so were they. For a couple of hours we could share our apprehension together. At about 10:00 A.M. things changed. I met my co-workers.

"College brat, ah." Such was the greeting I received from my new supervisor. He was a large man with a mean look in his eye. As I discovered later, he had learned his tactics in the navy when he had been in charge of inducting new recruits. I remember thinking that my worst nightmare had come true. It was as if I were back in the merchant marine waiting for the initiation ritual to begin. But then, something happened to change everything. Art stepped in.

Art had been watching me as the supervisor led me around and showed me the machine I was to run. Sensing my fear, Art walked up to the supervisor and offered to help train me. The supervisor made a gruff remark about not having the time to fool with me and accepted Art's offer. He made sure before he left to remind Art not to use this as an excuse to slack off his regular work. After the supervisor left, Art looked at me with a look that was as kind as the supervisor's look was mean. To put this into perspective, if I were to imagine a continuum from one to ten with meanness as one on the left and kindness as ten on the right, the supervisor was about a minus two whereas Art was a ten.

Once Art took over, my day improved. With Art's help, I learned how to run my machine and met several people in my work area. Things weren't altogether smooth. There was the usual tension that goes with joining a new group, but Art gave me the confidence to deal with making new relationships. Eventually, I became friends with several of the people in the area and even grew to like my work. I worked a machine that polished the finishing coat on computer disks. I took pride in finishing my disks to a smooth finish. I took pride in being part of our team. I learned that the disks coming out of our area were "on spec" more often than those of the other finishing areas. As fate would have it, however, the good times didn't last.

After several months on the finishing crew, I learned that Art was being transferred to a new area. We held a party for him. The party was fun, but an undercurrent of apprehension dampened the air. We all new that Art was the glue that held the group together. He was the true leader of the group. Art's leaving would change things.

Our apprehension proved right. After Art left, things went from bad to worse. Art was not replaced, a move prompted by the supervisor to cut costs. The supervisor took a more hands-on approach. He loved to bark commands and berate the weaker members of the group in front of their peers. And he was good at it. He knew the right buttons to push. The repercussions of this command-control style were felt rather immediately. Several members of our group began to call in sick as often as they could get away with it. Few took pride in their work. We polished our disks smoothly enough only to pass inspection. Arguments broke out frequently. When Art was away, we would release some of the pressure by engaging in "towel fights." We would wet the towels and throw them at each other. Throwing wet towels was the only fun left in our work. The rest of it was just "a job."

As I think back on my experience polishing disks, I am reminded of two truths. First, the encouragement and confirmation of one person can be a powerful force for creating personal power and bringing out productive relationships in a group. People who care at the right time help us get our wings flapping so that our spirits can take off again. On the other hand, one person's cruelty can destroy morale over night. The second truth of which I am reminded is that work is fun and productivity and quality are high when we feel good about our relationships with ourselves, our work, and each other.

Returning to the research with small work groups, we learn that this lesson from real life has a foundation in research. Bormann's work with small groups revealed that two critical hurdles a work group must cross are (1) to deal with primary tension and (2) to reach agreement on roles and relationships (Bormann 1990). Primary tension is the natural apprehension we have when we join a group. People deal with this in different ways. Some people laugh nervously, others come on strong, others hide in the corner. It is important for a group to have the right start, which means that people must be given the opportunity to release tension in ways that protect each member's self-esteem while moving the group toward the task. It is not unusual for a harmonizer like Art to step forward and help certain members of the group feel comfortable. Once primary tension is at a level where people are comfortable to move on, the role struggle begins.

Finding a meaningful role for each member is the most important process a work group goes through. Research and real-life experience shows that in groups in which some or all the members do not understand their role or are not satisfied with the role they have, the work does not get done and quality suffers. Based again on Bormann's research with small work groups, here's how role taking works (Bormann 1990).

First of all, roles emerge, they are not assigned. In truth, even when we assign roles, they often emerge differently. In the organization, we call the real roles, those that people actually practice, the *informal structure* to separate it from the formal structure that may or may not represent the functions actually performed and the relationships that develop between people. To relate this to my story, Art was likely the person who fulfilled the leader role. The formal supervisor was assigned by management to lead, but the followers thought differently. Which leads me to my second point: if allowed to follow a natural course, the followers decide who fits into what role, including the role of leader.

The aforementioned studies show not only that roles emerge from within the group but also that roles emerge from a process of residue. In other words, the person holding the role is the one who is left standing after the struggle for roles subsides. Bormann discovered two phases to the process of role emergence. In the first phase people "try out" for roles and either are encouraged by the group with gestures and comments of approval or are discouraged with frowns and comments of disapproval. The feedback of one's peers begins to shape the role one assumes in the group, albeit some people are more in tune with feedback than others are. Perhaps we all know of people who seem to continue to play a role in spite of the disapproval of the group. When this person is trying to play the role of leader, a painful struggle can result over who is the real leader. Other common roles for which people vie are (1) the leader's right-hand person (sometimes called lieutenant), (2) harmonizer, (3) task specialist, (4) devil's advocate, and (5) joker (sometimes called tension-releaser).

If the group is lucky, the first phase of role emergence ends with people in roles that fit their skills and aspirations and one person emerging as a leader. However, more often groups come out of phase one with some people happy in their role, others still vying for position, and more than one contender for leader. If the group does not find a meaningful role for everyone or if certain members feel slighted, the person without the role of his or her choosing retreats into silence or becomes an antagonist who undermines the work of the group whenever possible, what Bormann called "a central negative figure." In real life, a central negative figure can be a leader who knows he or she is not the natural leader chosen by the group and thus feels compelled to prove his or her power by taking it out on the weaker members of the group, or it can be someone inside the group who wanted to be leader but was not chosen and feels the constant need to put down both the work and the people. In either case, the bad apple sours the whole bunch.

If we look at the process of role emergence in the context of the model introduced earlier (Figure 13–1), we find that role finding is a process that goes on inside the group and a process that influences both the social and the task dimension of the group, proving once more that the two are connected.

If Bormann and others who study work groups are correct, role finding just might be the most critical process through which a work group must pass before people can engage in the task.

Relationships are important. At some level, I believe we all know this. Yet we continue to minimize the importance of relationships and to hide behind the task or the organization itself. "After all," we say, "the work must get done and the organization must be profitable and grow." I think—at least I hope—we are learning that healthy organizations are healthy only because they are made up of groups of people with healthy relationships with their work and each other. Groups like the one I described in my story are bad not only for people but also for the organization.

The issue of relationships at work is becoming more complicated every day. If for no other reason, we are being asked to work in multiple groups or teams. About the time we think we have settled into a meaningful role, we are moved to a new group. The "virtual community" that some people write about that forms across boundaries and disbands as quickly as it forms is a reality in the

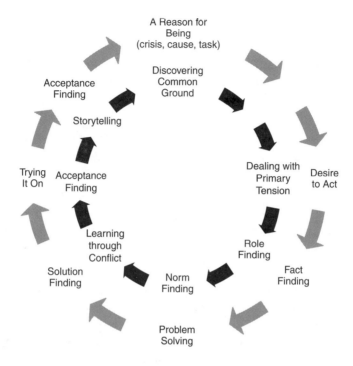

Figure 13–1   *The creative process expanded.*

workplace (Lipnack and Stamps 1993). In a world of virtual communities we need to be twice as good at working through the process of discovering meaningful roles and relationships than we ever were in an era of more stable structures. Granted, we have made progress. We have exposed some of the shadows of the industrial era and on the surface at least freed people to develop meaningful relationships at work. People are writing about relationships—even spiritual ones. Some of this talk has even permeated its way into the organization. When people are expected to jump from team to team, however, finding a meaningful role and nurturing relationships can be a real challenge.

Maybe we need to let go of our logic in order to understand roles and relationships at work. Maybe we should rely more on the analogical language of stories and metaphors such as gardening to understand relationships at work. Relationships are formed around the foundation of a shared reason for working together, such as the task of sowing seeds. They develop their own special rhythm as people work together with their hands, their heads, and their hearts. They grow to be healthy if people make a conscious commitment to hold a life and a task in common by paying attention to the morale of others, helping each other find meaningful roles, learning from the task and each other, and accepting conflict as part of the growth process.

Learning how to nurture healthy, caring relationships at work is indeed a big challenge. It helps to understand what goes on inside groups so that we can have a head start when dealing with the natural conflicts of life. It also helps to understand that we are all in this together and thus to discover common ground in our common human condition. Sometimes metaphors such as sowing seeds together in a garden help us appreciate the truth that relationships develop around a life and a task in common. In the process of developing understanding, common ground, and new interpersonal skills, it also helps to have the Arts of the world around—people who are there for other people as we all struggle to find meaningful roles and develop meaningful relationships.

14

Working the Soil Together

All work is important. All work is of value. The Amish honor what we would call the process *and* the product. BOTH. What I saw among the Amish was the amazing amount of energy available to people who get pleasure from what they are doing and find meaning in the work itself. But they are practical people who want that can of beans at the end of the day and the sixty-six jars of relish. For them it's all connected.

> . . . SUE BENDER *Plain and Simple*

There is joy in working together. This is another lesson I learned as a child gardener and have relearned from other gardeners I know. I used to love to make a game out of hoeing the garden. I would imagine myself opening the soil for the earth to catch its breath and for the roots to accept the moisture of coming rains. That the joy is in the work is a truth contained in the story about the children building sand castles on the beach (see chapter 7) and articulated by Sue Bender in the epigraph about her experience living in an Amish community (Bender 1989). Perhaps it is a lesson we would do well to apply more often in our formal organizations.

One of the simple lessons I learned while searching for community at work was that community forms around the practical tasks in life, the can of beans, the sixty-six jars of relish, the vegetables in the garden. Those who have studied creativity have discovered a similar truth. The creative process is stimulated by a real event, often a crisis. Creativity blossoms when people gather facts, engage in problem solving, and work on solutions. Not that it has to be serious business. On the contrary, people are the most creative when work is play. The anthropologist Edward Hall reminds us that people, like other animals, learn through play. Citing the work of A.R. Luria on the human brain, Hall pointed out that body movement and problem solving both are controlled by the frontal part of the brain and therefore are connected. In Hall's words: "Who would have thought that body movement was related to problem solving?" (Hall 1976, p. 199). So maybe throwing toys around in a business meeting is not a dumb idea after all.

Csikszentmihalyi's (1990) discoveries made while observing people lost in the "flow" of their work substantiate the same simple truth: people are happiest when they are engaged in completing a task or accomplishing a goal. Happiness and joy are in the practical and simple things of life.

I learned this simple truth from the opposite side by working in groups that had no purpose. I recall being part of an executive steering team whose supposed purpose was to oversee a quality movement. Everyone in the group had a different idea of what the group should do. We wrestled with a charter for five meetings, only to find that the one we drafted was rejected by half the group. To make a long story short, the group never did decide why they were a group let alone what they should work on.

Russell Eisenstat wrote about a similar experience with a team of managers whose task was to coordinate a plant start-up (Hackman 1990). As it turned out, the group was never certain of its role. While the management group was going to meetings trying to decide what to do, the workers in the plant got the job done. The group eventually disbanded, leaving its members soured on teams that hurt the company's efforts regarding quality.

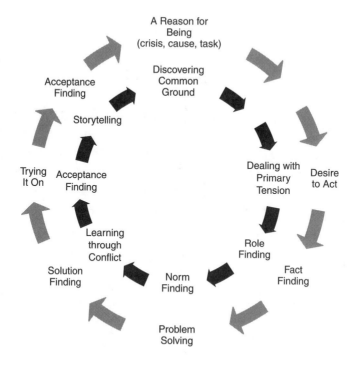

Figure 14–1 *The creative process expanded.*

Fortunately, there are groups even in the formal organization who seem to have learned this simple truth that the joy is in the task. I was blessed to be part of one when I worked in the Division That Cared. The story about the people who grew vegetables is about a group who cared in the middle of an organization that cared only about growth and profits. The central message of this book is that caring relationships around common tasks is what we need to cultivate.

Perhaps the little game I played as a child in the garden imagining that my hoe was breaking the ground so that the plants could breathe and accept moisture from the rain (which is not far from what actually happens) carries a message for the organization even beyond the simple message that the joy is in the task. I would like to think it does. When we work together around a common task, such as cultivating the ground, working the soil together, we open ourselves up to new relationships. We allow ourselves the opportunity to discover common ground. As we work and play together using our imaginations as well as our intellects, we learn that the joy is in the task.

The creative model in Figure 14–1 shows that fact finding, problem solving, and solution finding are a large part of the task dimension. All this takes place, however, in the context of the social-relationship dimension of role finding, agreeing on acceptable behavior toward the task and each other (norms), and learning through conflict, which leads me to the next chapter.

15

Growing through Conflict

Community is not opposed to conflict. On the contrary, community is precisely that place where an arena for creative conflict is protected by the compassionate fabric of human caring itself.

... PARKER J. PALMER
Community, Conflict, and Ways of Knowing

Clearing out old assumptions about relationships at work and discovering common ground around a meaningful task and a life together go a long way toward building strong relationships at work. But they do not prevent conflict from emerging—often just when we expect it the least. Even gardens are not free of conflict.

After thirty years living inside the organization and listening to others who work in government, education, religion, health care, and business organizations, I have reached the conclusion that people in the United States are, for the most part, lousy at dealing with conflict. The reason lies in our win-lose assumptions articulated in chapter 9. Some people avoid conflict at all costs whereas others revel in it like sharks after a wounded dolphin.

Conflict is part of life. It starts at birth with the difficult journey from the safety and comfort of the womb into a strange, cold world. Those who are fortunate find themselves loved and protected by parents who care for them. But even the love and care of good parents does not make us immune to the trials and tribulations of life. As the great child psychologist Erik Erikson revealed, growing up means dealing with the natural conflict of life and taking on an identity of our own while others around us take on one of their own, often quite different form ours (Erikson 1980). That is not by any means an easy thing to do, as every caring parent knows.

Later we learn that conflict doesn't stop when we grow up. There is no conflict-free place where we can hide from life. There is no garden where we can escape from the need to know and to grow, a truth revealed in creation stories such as that of Adam and Eve in the Bible, who were not satisfied in the protective environment of the Garden of Eden. Their need for knowledge and growth represented by the beguiling serpent mirrored what we all go through when we eat the fruit of knowledge. We discover that the tree of knowledge is full of stuff we didn't necessarily want to know, as the knowledge that life is about dying as well as birthing. So even gardens aren't safe from the realities of life. Let's face it, the old Portuguese proverb, "die young or suffer much," may be rather blunt, but it tells a truth about life that is hard to deny.

There is another, more optimistic truth about conflict. We become persons through conflict. To look at this from the opposite end, if we avoid or repress conflict, we do not grow. It would be wonderful to stay in the warmth and protection of the womb or remain in the loving care of our family, but we would not be happy, for to do so would be to stop growing. There is something in all of us that propels us forward. As Erikson revealed, we are destined to deal with the conflicts that are part of becoming a person with a unique identity of our very own, but we are also given the opportunity to learn and grow by dealing with the natural conflicts of life in healthy, "becoming" ways.

Conflict is also part of our relationships. It doesn't take us long to discover as we grow that others have differing opinions from ours or that they may look at the world from an entirely different angle. On the basis of our win-lose view of conflict, we see these differences as threats. Differences are also an opportunity to learn and grow. President Lyndon Johnson put this simple truth into plain talk: "we don't learn much by listening to ourselves."

If conflict is a natural part of the process of becoming persons with healthy relationships, then maybe the problem is not conflict itself. Maybe the problem is the way we look at conflict. Maybe we need to challenge our basic assumption about what conflict means and how it affects people and changes the very rules of the game. Maybe conflict is not a win-lose, lose-lose game. Maybe conflict is an opportunity to learn, gain new insight, and become whole persons with healthy relationships. If we look at conflict in this new light, it takes on a new meaning.

As Adam and Eve of the ancient myth discovered, even gardens are not an escape from the natural conflict of life, including the conflict that emerges when people work together side by side. It helps to discover common ground while cultivating our gardens, but it does not stop people from asserting their power or egos from being bruised. The key is to look at conflict as an opportunity to learn and to grow both as persons and as groups. But how does one go about a change of such magnitude? "After all," you might say, "our entire culture is infested with the win-lose, lose-lose paradigm; it's not just at work."

Sometimes the best way to tackle a difficult issue is to start with a story. The following story was told to me by a frustrated manager who learned that conflict could be a source for learning and growth. But he learned it like most lessons in life—through conflict itself.

The day that Jim was appointed manager of the newly formed by-products division, he knew that he was in for a big challenge. Jim had worked with some of the people in the division, just enough to know about the ongoing feuds. He had inadvertently witnessed a couple of the battles as a member of a cross-functional team. What he didn't know about was the role that he was destined to play.

Two days after the announcement was made that Jim would manage the division, Sue approached him. She informed him that the group was riddled with conflict and that she was glad that he was there to fix it. Jim accepted her comments with a grain of salt, knowing from experience that conflict was never quite as simple as it appeared on the surface and that fixing it was going to be much more difficult than Sue imagined. Jim's intuition told him that the conflict probably had deep roots and branches that spread out into many places. At the first meeting with his staff Jim learned that his intuition was correct.

The first management staff meeting with Jim at the helm started very politely. Jim was welcomed with open arms. Each of the people who reported directly to Jim took his or her turn to tell Jim why his skills were just what they needed and to express a commitment to supporting Jim's efforts. But the polite atmosphere was destined to die with the introduction of the first issue of the day. Paul, the operations director, announced that costs were up because of raw material costs, which would result in a negative variance. Sue, the administrative director, interrupted Paul before he could finish his analysis of the issue and pointed out that her purchasing manager could have bought raw materials at a much better cost if only she had received "good production forecasts." Paul jumped back into the conversation quickly with a comment about Mary's "lousy sales numbers" and soon the argument was in full swing. It ended abruptly when Jim starting asking for a recap of the events. At that point, no one wanted to talk about it anymore.

The pattern observed by Jim at his first staff meeting repeated itself over and over again in the months that followed. Jim observed that Sue often triggered the arguments. Some of the battles grew so heated that the entire division was singed in the process. The hall talk had it that Jim's staff was out of control. Jim knew that he must do something.

Jim's first move was to face the issue head on. He announced to his staff that the conflict was hurting their ability to work together as a team, and consequently the quality of their work was suffering. Jim told them that as the leaders of the division they must stop this childish behavior and set an example for the rest of the division. For a while things cooled down. But Jim started receiving complaints from others outside of his staff that the conflict had not gone away. It had merely moved out into the office and the plant. After several complaints, Jim knew that he needed to try something else.

Jim's next move was to consult with the human resources department. After listening to Jim, the vice president of human resources suggested that Jim send Sue to an intensive personal development program that included a segment on interpersonal competence and conflict management. After all, she seemed to be the one who instigated the episodes of conflict. Jim followed this advice and after a painful session with Sue got her to agree to enroll in the program as part of her learning plan.

For several weeks things calmed down. Everyone was encouraged by Sue's willingness to work on the problem and was relieved that the problem was not them. But the false peace was as short-lived as the previous episodes of calm were. Other members of the staff started taking stabs at each other. Sue stayed out of it at first. As the bickering continued, Sue saw it as an opportunity to use her new-found knowledge and skills in interpersonal communication and conflict management. She would tell the others when they were doing things wrong and show them how to interact in more healthy ways. Her help was welcomed with as much enthusiasm as an army of ants at a summer picnic. Paul articulated the feelings of the group well (at least according to the group) when he told Sue to keep her "better-than-thou" opinions to herself. After a brief cold war of only talking about business mixed with vicious nonverbal gestures, Jim found himself back at the drawing board.

Jim's next move happened more by accident than by design. It started with insight as opposed to another program from the outside. The insight Jim needed to understand the conflict that ate away at the relationships within the division and interfered with their work came as a result of an informal chat with the marketing director, Debbie. Jim was lamenting the situation and wondering out loud how it had become so bad in the first place. Debbie didn't know why things had gotten out of hand. She only knew that it all started right after the last manager was appointed. She reflected on how Sue had expected to be named manager and how disappointed she had been when she didn't get the job. Sue was even more disappointed to discover later that her peers had not supported her bid for manager because they thought her style was too abrupt. In other words, Sue felt abandoned by her peers, having expected them to back her. Sue had never gotten over being wounded and seemed to take it out on the rest of the group, especially Paul, whenever she could. According to Debbie's assessment, after that the group seemed to thrive on conflict. It became a way of life with Sue as the perpetrator; Paul, the victim; Mary, the rescuer; and Debbie trying to bring harmony back.

As his conversation with Debbie progressed, Jim began to realize that he was witnessing only the symptoms. The conflict had deep roots that were embedded in the history of the group. Jim also realized that conflict is something that rests with the entire group, not just an individual or two people who are bickering. Indeed, as Debbie wisely observed, conflict becomes a way of life, a ritual of sorts. To deal with conflict and learn through it, the entire group must own it and be willing to take the time to understand its roots and to empathize with each other. Once Jim began to approach the problem from this deeper and broader perspective, slowly but surely the group moved out of their destructive pattern of personal put-downs and learned to disagree with each other with respect for each other.

With the help of a trained facilitator, the group learned to understand why Sue felt the way she did and how they all contributed to the rituals that kept them trapped in a vicious circle of fight-or-flight behavior. They didn't stop disagreeing or stop dealing with difficult issues. On the contrary, the group was very noisy at times. But they learned to disagree, to welcome differences, in the spirit of openness, learning, and respect for each person. For example, when they disagreed or when one of the group wanted to assert an opposite opinion, he or she always made certain to address the issue and the facts surrounding it. In fact, one of the rules the group adapted was that no one could disagree before restating the other's opinion to that person's satisfaction. The group began to see conflict as a natural part of learning and growing. In the process they learned to accept and care for each other. In the end, they viewed the unhealthful put-down rituals they had been stuck in as a significant event in the history of their group. They would talk about how they grew from conflict and how it made their relationships stronger and their work more productive. For Jim's group, conflict became a bonding event as opposed to a source of stress and entropy. The group knew it could weather the next storm of conflict all the stronger for having lived and learned through dealing with conflict openly in the spirit of learning.

Jim's story had a happy ending. Many stories with similar plots do not. In truth, it would be naive to assume that all conflict can be turned into a learning experience. In reality, there are groups that never get out of their vicious put-down rituals, and there are people who seem to revel in conflict, going after a more sensitive member of the group like a shark after a wounded dolphin. In more severe cases, the shark must be forced to leave before the group can function. Fortunately, there are other groups that, like Jim's group, learn from conflict. There are lessons to be learned from both.

In addition to the experiences of groups like Jim's and of others that not have ended so happily, we can learn from models and programs offered to help us understand and deal with conflict. The plethora of models and programs available are beyond what can be reviewed here. However, they can be grouped into four approaches: (1) the skills approach, (2) the systems approach, (3) the psychoanalytic approach, and (4) the process approach.

The Skills Approach

The skills approach is based on the assumption that we will manage conflict better if we learn certain basic interpersonal skills. Usually the person or group is presented new skills and an opportunity to practice them. In an article in *The Speech Teacher*, Arthur Bochner and Clifford Kelly, two professors of communication, summarized years of research into five basic skills: (1) *empathetic communication*, the "ability to take the role of the other," (2) *descriptiveness*, or the ability to describe the issue and the facts and give clear feedback without attacking the person, (3) *owning feelings and thoughts*, the willingness to take responsibility for one's feelings and actions rather than blame others, (4) *self disclosure*, the willingness to voluntarily share with others things about oneself that the other is unlikely to know while respecting the privacy of others, and (5) *behavioral flexibility*, being willing to change behavior and try on new ways of dealing with differences constructively (Bochner and Kelly 1974).

Learning basic interpersonal skills like those identified by Bochner and Kelly can be valuable and can indeed improve communications, but as Jim discovered the entire group must learn them together if the intent is to resolve a bitter feud. If only one member is exposed to these new skills, he or she can be viewed in a better-than-thou light. The other issue in skills development is that it deals primarily with symptoms and often does not get at the root of the problem. It is like telling the doctor that it hurts to move your arm a certain way and being told in response, "just don't move it that way." For new skills to take hold, the group must dig a little deeper into the causes and effects.

The Systems Approach

The second major approach to conflict management is the systems approach. Here the idea is to look at conflict as a series of actions and reactions. Often the group is encouraged to map out its behavior to see what is going on and to better understand why each person involved might see the conflict in a different cause-effect pattern. For example, in one case study a rather quiet member of a group who was accused of not speaking out reported that she felt intimidated by an aggressive member of the group, which was why she did not speak up. When confronted with the situation, the aggressive member was surprised. From his angle, he needed to be aggressive because the quiet member of the group needed his encouragement. The pattern went like this: She is quiet because he is aggressive; he is aggressive because she is quiet. Karl Weick's work with vicious circles and double binds showed how certain behaviors elicit specific responses and can actually amplify unhealthy conflict and misunderstandings

(Weick 1979). It has been used effectively by groups to increase understanding.

Chris Argyris has taken a systems approach to the organization (Argyris 1993). Looking at conflict from a systems perspective of cause and effect and deviant amplifying cycles goes farther than the skills approach in helping people understand how conflict works and why it is the property of the entire group and not just select individuals, but it can fall short of getting at the emotional issues. In fact, one of the criticisms of systems thinking is that it emphasizes the rational to the extent that it overshadows the reality that rational behavior depends on emotional responses from people with limits to their ability to understand everything that is going on and who have feelings that get in the way. Argyris noted this limitation when he identified embarrassment as a major obstacle to overcome before people were willing to deal with conflict.

The Psychoanalytic Approach

The psychoanalytic approach differs from the other approaches in that it goes after the roots of conflict. In this approach one assumes that bringing hidden motives and unconscious assumptions to a conscious level will help set people free from vicious circles of unhealthy conflict. In other words, just knowing that our behavior is destructive will help us change at a deeper level. The classic work of British psychoanalyst Wilfred Bion at the Tavistock Clinic is an example of this approach (Bormann 1990).

Bion identified three patterns of group behavior that if allowed to remain unconscious can consume the group and cause dysfunctional behavior. His work was based on the theory that there are two aspects to every group. The work group is one; the other he called the basic assumption group. Basic assumption means exactly what it says, the assumption is basic to the behavior. It is an "as if" term. One behaves as if such and such were the case. A basic assumption group operates at a tacit level and often at a subconscious level. Bion named three basic assumption groups: dependency, fight-or-flight, and pairing.

A dependency group acts as if they are totally dependent on a strong leader or organization. Members of dependency groups can be heard saying, "If only we had some real leadership around here." Fight-or-flight groups act just as their label says, as if one is against the other, as did Sue and Paul in Jim's group, or the group against the world, as do groups bound up in a siege mentality. Pairing groups act as if they have met for one overriding reason: to produce a messiah or savior. But any messiah that does appear is quickly rejected because the purpose of the group is to live in anticipation and hope. You can hear members make comments such as "When such and such happens or so and so comes everything will be great." Bion pointed out that every group operates with these assumptions at a tacit level. The secret is to be aware of the basic assumption so that the group can make mature decisions about its behavior.

Bion made the important point that basic assumption groups lie in the unconsciousness of every group. An awareness of this helps a group operate in the real world conscious of the basic assumptions that are shaping its behavior and causing unproductive conflict. Leadership plays an important role in Bion's theory. In the naive or unconscious fantasy, the leader of the dependency group has to be omnipotent; the fight leader unbeatable and the flight leader uncatchable; the leader of the pairing group must be marvelous but still unborn. In the mature conscious group, which is aware of and making a sophisticated use of the appropriate basic assumptions, the dependency group is dependable; the leader of the fight-or-flight group is courageous; and the leader of the pairing group is creative. Furthermore, groups who are aware of their basic assumptions have a better chance at learning how to use the natural conflicts of life as learning and growing experiences.

Bion is not the only one to develop a theory around achieving a level of awareness. M. Scott Peck's model of group consciousness raising gets at the same process (Peck 1987). The parallel to the psychoanalysis of unconscious impulses is clear. Presumably, the more the basic assumption life of the group reaches a conscious level, the more effectively the group functions as a group in their shared task.

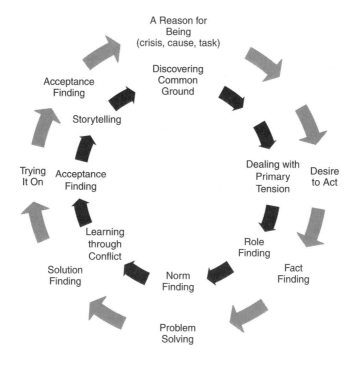

A Reason for
Being
(crisis, cause, task)

Discovering
Common
Ground

Acceptance
Finding

Storytelling

Dealing with
Primary
Tension

Desire
to Act

Trying
It On

Acceptance
Finding

Learning
through
Conflict

Role
Finding

Fact
Finding

Solution
Finding

Norm
Finding

Problem
Solving

Figure 15–1 *The creative process expanded.*

The Process Approach

The process approach to conflict incorporates the other three approaches and adds the process to the formula. Perhaps the best way to get at this approach is to return to the model of community building at work (Figure 15–1).

As the model shows, the inner life of the group involves dealing with and growing through conflict while the outer circle connects the inner life of the group to the shared task that holds the group together. The point to be reinforced is that conflict is part of the life of a group. Some might say there is no other way for work groups to become effective, caring communities without learning how to grow through conflict. M. Scott Peck made this point clear in his book on community when he asserted that the only way to

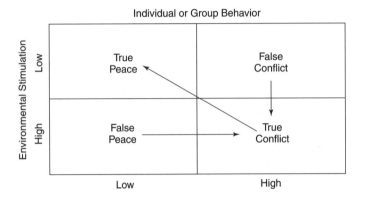

Figure 15–2 *Peace and conflict. (Source: Thomas Fiutak)*

community is through chaos and emptiness (Peck 1987). In Peck's view, work groups must be willing to bring the shadows of their dysfunctional behavior into the open and lose their false sense of community (what he refers to as pseudo-community) to discover real community.

Robert Terry sheds light on the process of dealing with conflict with a simple model adapted from the work of Thomas Fiutak, associate director at the Center for Conflict and Change at the University of Minnesota (Terry 1993). In Terry's model (Figure 15–2) there is no shortcut to true peace. One must first go through and learn from conflict. The lesson here is that conflict is not a bad thing to be avoided. Healthy groups in which people care for each other and the task are places where it is safe to deal with conflict without the fear of being put down. Healthy groups also discover that dealing with conflict in ways that respect the individual and the group can be a source of bonding.

Bormann calls the process of building a cohesive work group a *symbolic convergence* to emphasize the point that shared histories, including learning through episodes of conflict, become shared symbols that hold the group together (Bormann 1990). Conflict, if dealt with openly and with care for the individual as well as the group, can help a group of individuals become a community at work with a life and a task in common.

Summary

Conflict is part of living. It emerges from the natural fears described in Part II of this book. Even gardeners cannot escape it. If viewed as a win-lose game or if denied as though life should be free of it, conflict can get out of hand and rear its ugly head in the form of personal put-downs, pouting, denial, and other forms of unhealthy behavior that ultimately produce stress. If like Jim's group, we are tempted to place the blame on a person or a specific situation and seek quick fixes, we will likely miss the deeper roots of conflict and its ritual and process-oriented nature.

In truth, every work group has its own rhythm and ways of dealing with conflict. Learning to understand conflict as part of the rhythm of a life and a task in common is the secret to creating a productive group in which people find joy in their work and grow as individuals while the work gets done. Groups that have learned this valuable lesson have a rhythm of their own that includes learning through conflict. Like the gardener who learns to cooperate with the forces of nature, even when the forces temporarily cause havoc, the group that learns through conflict learns to grow in harmony with its work and each other.

16

Living in Harmony

> Perhaps this is the most important thing for me to take back
> from beach-living: simply the memory that each cycle of the
> tide is valid; each cycle of the wave is valid; each cycle of a
> relationship is valid.
>
> . . . ANNE MORROW LINDBERGH *Gift from the Sea*

Relationships have a rhythm like the rhythm of the tides or the
rhythm of the gardener who has learned to let the hoe do the work.
But this rhythm can get out of synch like the tide in a storm or the
hoe that lets its master's anger take over. The storms of conflict can
take on a life of their own, as we discovered in chapter 15, and wreak
havoc for a time. As we also found in chapter 15, there is much to
learn from the storms of life. Perhaps the first lesson is that cultivating common ground while holding a life and a task in common is
about learning from the storms of life and discovering the rhythm
of the group in the process.

The most profound truths about life are often lodged in simple
concepts that seem to emerge again and again across cultures and
endure over time. One of those enduring concepts is *harmony*. In his
book *The Evolving Self* Mihaly Csikszentmihalyi asserts that Western

cultures often define harmony as the absence of conflict, but that is not the kind of harmony that makes groups work and societies flourish (Csikszentmihalyi 1993). On the contrary, the concept of harmony that defines species that learn, survive, and flourish is more synonymous with complexity. As such, it welcomes conflict as part of learning. Harmony is discovered in the rhythms of life that swing from differentiation to integration. It is the pattern discovered by developmental psychologists in the rhythm of a person's life from birth to adulthood to death and all of the conflict and transitions in between. It is a rhythm that students of interaction have discovered in conflict itself as people establish points of difference and integrate them back into the whole.

To get my arms around this simple, yet profound concept, I introduce another simple model based on the work of Robert Bales and others who have studied the rhythm of cohesive work groups (Bales 1970) (Figure 16–1).

The vertical axis of the model measures the level of tension or conflict in the group. The horizontal axis measures the group's history. Initially the tension is high because of the normal tension associated with getting to know people. For that reason it is called *primary tension.* Primary tension is usually tempered with jokes, nervous gestures, and other rituals that put people at ease and bring the level of tension to the level at which the group is free to put their energy to the task. If, however, the group fails to deal with the primary tension that arises early, later when people try to find roles and deal with differences, a tension with deeper roots called *secondary tension* rears its ugly head.

In Jim's story in chapter 15, secondary tension is what Sue and Paul manifested in their behavior. Its roots are frequently lodged in the struggle to be leader or in different world views. In the life of a community at work, people are bound to feel misunderstood, slighted, ignored, embarrassed, or kept from playing a significant role from time to time. If the group does not learn how to deal with these and other sources of conflict in an open spirit of learning, unresolved secondary tension can keep the group from working effectively on the task. As the model shows, the group goes above its

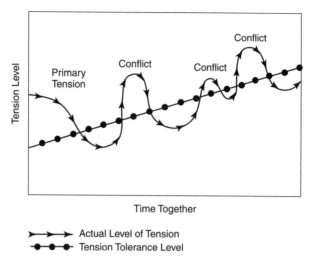

Figure 16–1 *Conflict and tension.*

tension tolerance level. On the other hand, if the level of tension is too low, the group may not experience conflict, but it also may not get anything done. The "right" level of tension keeps the group productive. It also encourages growth through conflict. The dotted line in Figure 16–1 shows that as the group deals with conflict, its tolerance of tension increases and so does its ability to work on the task.

This model like all models tries to capture things that one can not capture on paper. But at least it helps us understand that conflict is part of the rhythm of a group. Contrary to what we have been encouraged to believe, healthy groups are not places where everyone goes out of their way to avoid confrontation and conflict. In truth, healthy groups are noisy groups. They move from accenting differences to integrating them into the whole in a harmony that encourages each member to sing in solo and in chorus.

A return to Figure 16–2 and the creative process shows that healthy groups pay attention to the task and to the relationships between members of the group, both the outer and the inner life of the group.

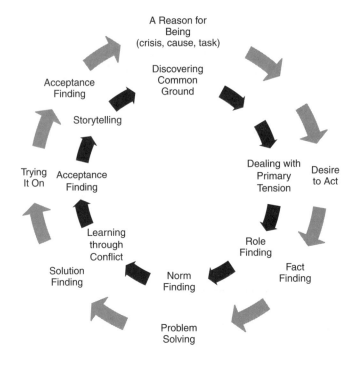

Figure 16–2   *The creative process expanded.*

In reality, every community at work must find its own rhythm. Some groups spend time at the beginning of every day talking about relationships. Other groups do it when the spirit moves them. Truly healthy groups blend relationships into their work to the extent that one observing them cannot tell the difference. They fill the needs of the members of the group who are more task-oriented by nature and of those who are oriented more toward relationships. The important point is that the group recognize the need to pay attention to relationships and to help each other as the need arises if it truly wishes to become a community at work.

There is another truth about harmony and community that we would do well to ponder before moving on. Not every day working together is as wonderful or as bad as the day before. The rhythm of a community at work involves times of stress and confusion and

Four-room Apartment

Contentment	Renewal
Denial	Confusion

Figure 16–3   *The four-room apartment.*

times when everything seems to go smoothly. Some days cultivating the ground is hard work—we can't wait to leave it and go home. On other days there is no place on earth we would rather be than in our gardens cultivating common ground with our friends. This simple truth is captured in a model Weisbord (1992) calls the four-room apartment (Figure 16–3). It can just as easily be called four gardens.

The point of the model is that one day we might find ourselves in the garden of contentment, where life and work seem to flow with ease, as encountered by a gardener lost in the art of planting. On another day, it could be the very next day, we struggle in the garden of confusion, where the weeds are so thick we cannot see our way around or through them. On yet another day we linger in the garden of denial, unwilling to deal with conflict for fear of losing ourselves. Then, there are the days when we sense a renewal. Usually they follow a day when we have dealt openly with our feelings and learned through our differences. Because we know what it is like to work in the garden of confusion and denial, we can experience the joy of renewal whereas otherwise we would not. Once again, we renew our conscious commitment to holding a life and a task in common, knowing full well that we will find ourselves cultivating in a row of confusion and denial but knowing also that we will experience renewal and contentment again. Perhaps life is like that.

Work groups that bring out the power of caring relationships promote harmony, at times focusing on differences in the spirit of dialogue and learning, at other times integrating these differences into the whole. In the process they discover a rhythm of their own as they prepare for the harvest of their labors.

17

Celebrating the Harvest

We may get to the point where our external labors and the
opus of the soul are one and the same, inseparable. Then the
satisfactions of our work will be deep and long lasting, undone
neither by failures nor by flashes of success.

> . . . THOMAS MOORE *Care of the Soul*

There is joy in gardening. There is even more joy in gardening together. And it culminates in the joy of the harvest.

Our basic assumptions about work and relationships have
been keeping us from experiencing the real joy of the harvest. By
forcing relationships underground, avoiding intimacy, bullying our
way through conflict or repressing it away, we have robbed ourselves of a source of energy that makes communities at work both
productive and a joy to work in. It is time we learned how to celebrate again.

Fortunately, not everyone forgot the joy of the harvest. Not
long ago a friend of mine shared her joy of the harvest with me. She
told me about a group with whom she worked who celebrated their
accomplishments with a ceremony. A large community candle was
placed in the center of a circle. Each member of the work group took

a turn lighting his or her own candle from the community candle while sharing their most significant experience while working on the task. At the end of the ceremony the group held hands and sang a folk song about the value of learning and growing together.

But don't we celebrate enough already? At least that is what some people in the organization tell me. I am reminded by them that we celebrate frequently at the corner bar or on the softball field. I must agree with them. People do seem to get together after work regularly. I also agree that these social activities are good for relationships. But I know that many of these celebrations do not always include those who performed the work, such as the sales meeting that excludes the customer service department or the stop-off at the bar that excludes those who do not indulge. Furthermore, my experience is that these rituals seldom bring out the true joy of the harvest. More often, they turn into gripe sessions during which people accent their differences without integrating them into solutions that will help relationships grow. Not that gripe sessions are bad. In truth, they can be very healthy ways to vent frustrations. For complaints to turn into solutions, however, they must deal openly with the facts and find ways to engage all the people on common ground.

Perhaps this is one area where we can learn from our ancestors. And we may not have to go that far back. The story "The Harvest" at the end of Part I is about threshing crews in the 1940s. But in many ways these virtual communities that got together once a year to harvest oats were much like the teams that now run around the new organization. They formed quickly around a task in common and changed membership as they moved from farm to farm. At the beginning and sometimes at the end of the harvest the threshing crew would gather together and share a large meal or an ice cream social. They would talk of the task and release the tension that had not been resolved as they worked side by side to bring the grain off the land. If we go back even farther, we discover rituals of the harvest that included fire and dance. Our ancestors knew much about the value of celebrating the harvest.

I am happy to note that in my search for community at work I have discovered a resurrection of celebration rituals. I know of several consultants who are helping organizations rediscover the role of rituals in the process of change, not only for celebrating the harvest but also for grieving loss. In a time of rapid change in which people are not sure of their footing, the value of rituals is immeasurable.

Celebrating the harvest can serve several purposes, not the least of which is the sheer joy of the celebration itself. There is only one joy greater than the joy of a job well done: the joy of a job well done together. It has benefits that go beyond the celebration itself. The energy it produces can spill over to the next task in either the same group or a new community that is ready to form.

A celebration marks the ending of one episode and the beginning of another. So it is with this book. I must end this journey through the life of a community at work and move on to the final part of the book on relationships and the new organization. Before I move on I must make one important point, perhaps the most important point of all.

Building a community at work requires a conscious commitment. As my friend James Frank Mossman reminded me, it is about "holding a life and a task in common" which means that relationships are at the core of the community. This is not an easy task. But it is a rewarding one. And what makes this task possible? Parker Palmer (1977, p. 25) said it best when he wrote: "The only answer I can give is that what makes community possible is love." With that thought fresh on our minds and warm in our hearts, I invite you to join me in the final part of this book for a look at caring communities of the future. But I must warn you. You might get caught in the joy of cultivating common ground together. Like John in the story at the end of Part I of this book, your life could change forever.

IV

Relationships and the New Organization

Change comes from small initiatives which, imitated, become the fashion. We cannot wait for great visions from great people, for they are in short supply at the end of history. It is up to us to light our own small fires in the darkness.

... CHARLES HANDY *The Age of Paradox*

18

*The People Discover
New Gardens*

The years passed. All but two of the people who once grew vegetables in the Great Kingdom had moved on. The Knight of Reengineering had left the Great Kingdom long ago. In truth, his popularity had waned throughout the land. His message was being drowned out by new concepts such as learning organizations, transformation, and spirituality at work. In reality, there were so many programs that the people who worked in the Great Kingdom had grown confused and tired from reading books and going to seminars. They longed for life to come back to order. As for the people who once grew vegetables, they just wanted to get back to caring for their work and each other.

Every now and then, the people who grew vegetables would gather at the local restaurant to talk about the old days. It was there that they learned that the seeds of caring that had been planted in the Great Kingdom years before had landed on new soil. Some had even taken root and were producing new gardens where people were learning to care for their work and each other.

Ralph, who had been the first victim of the Knight of Reengineering, had joined a group of consultants who were dedicated to helping others find work. He shared his joy over helping several of the people who grew vegetables find gardens where people cared for their work and each other. It was through Ralph that they learned about Sandra, one of the best planters the group had ever known. She had joined with two of the growers from their group, George and Philip, to form a new cooperative dedicated to growing vegetables using only natural methods. Their business was small, but they were able to serve a thriving community near the city and generate enough profit to provide for themselves and five others. They were busy practicing the same caring ways they had nurtured in the Great Kingdom.

Janet had discovered that her gift for helping people learn how to grow from dealing with conflict openly could be used to help others learn from their differences. She worked in a neighboring kingdom that in reality was not a kingdom at all. The enterprise was made up of self-managed work groups that had been put together by a group of trustees to grow fruits and vegetables. Janet's role was to help the groups develop and share learning experiences. She was busy helping each group learn from the others and enjoying her role. She was able to bring several of the people who grew vegetables into the new enterprise.

As for the two people who remained in the Great Kingdom, life was not so bad after all. It seems that the morale of the people was not the only thing to drop. Profits also had tumbled. As the profits tumbled so did the esteem of the king in the eyes of the people. Eventually, the king grew so frustrated he left. He was replaced with a new leader. She brought with her new ways of working. She redesigned the structure of the Great Kingdom around autonomous work units. One of the work units was structured based on the model set by the people who grew vegetables.

As fate would have it, the two people who were left from the original people who grew vegetables emerged as leaders in the new work unit. They were able to practice their caring ways once again. The caring spread and before long a new group of people who grew vegetables were busy cultivating common ground, caring for their work and each other. They often told stories about the first group with fondness and were grateful for the seeds of caring that had grown and blossomed in their own group.

Thus, the people who grew vegetables never really died. Their caring ways spread far and wide as caring ways do. Perhaps they will spread to your workplace and to mine.

19

The Changing Workplace

To live in a quantum world, to weave here and there with ease
and grace, we will need to change what we do. We will need to
stop describing tasks and instead facilitate *process*. We will need
to become savvy about how to build relationships, how to
nurture growing, evolving things.

. . . MARGARET J. WHEATLEY
Leadership and the New Science

As the people who grew vegetables discovered, the world of work
is changing, including the way we structure our organizations. They
also discovered that these new structures can be turned into opportunities to spread caring ways into new communities at work.
Granted, the people who grew vegetables are make-believe, but
maybe we can still learn from them that caring is contagious.

The world of work is changing. But some things change slowly.
Or perhaps they never change. Like our tendency to work in groups.
In a book about the modern "networked" organization, Jessica Lip-
nack and Jeffrey Stamps reminded us of an old truth about change
(Lipnack and Stamps 1993). Change is cumulative. In other words,
the old is not suddenly replaced with the new. Often it is piled on

top of the old. This truth applies to organizational structures. Figure 19–1 shows the organizational structures that have emerged over four eras.

In addition to the truth that structures are never completely replaced, the model also shows that the small work group is one of the oldest forms of organizing. Furthermore, the small work group is still an integral part of the organization, a truth that should come as no surprise to those who live inside the organization. In the final analysis, organizations are and always have been made up of groups of work groups. Some of them operate as groups of people who care for their work and each other much like the people who grew vegetables operated. Perhaps it was only at the top of the hierarchical structures that we were fooled into thinking that the organization was a living organism supported by a few loyal individuals who kept tabs on the rest of the troops—and that caring was out of order. Without question, people have been working in groups and caring for each other for a long time.

Nevertheless, organizations are changing. As Figure 19–1 also shows, the small work group may be the oldest form and what holds the organization together, but it is not the only form. Over the years we have added hierarchies, bureaucracies, and more recently, teams and networks, or what Lipnack and Stamps call *teamnets*. No wonder life in the organization is confusing these days.

In the new organization work groups will likely still be around. Only many of them will form quickly and change membership just as quickly as they formed. To be sure, there will be teams and networks and teamnets, but there also will be work groups that stay together for a period of time. In other words, there will be both real work communities that work together for months and even years and virtual work communities that form for only brief periods of time to accomplish a specific task around a specific purpose, as people gather in the community garden and leave to join other groups at work. Many people will move from garden to garden. Some organizations will merely provide a plot on which to grow a garden for a season. The challenge is to find ways to build caring relationships in the middle of it all.

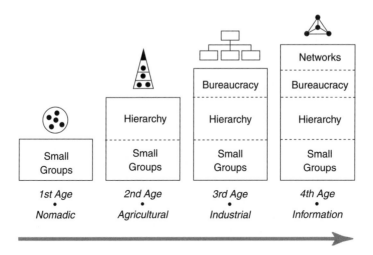

Figure 19–1   *Building capabilities.*

As the story about the harvest in Part I revealed, even virtual communities are not totally new. Threshing crews and sewing clubs have been around for years. Maybe they offer valuable lessons about nurturing community around a life and a task in common. And maybe the most valuable lesson of them all is that we must make it happen. The organization won't do it for us. As I have said over and over again, caring communities at work emerge only when real people make a conscious commitment to holding a life and a task in common.

Throughout this book I have suggested that caring relationships at work never really went away. They merely went underground for a period of time. The Hawthorne studies at the Western Electric plant revealed that on the shop floor where products and people touched each other, people were caring for their work and each other all along—even at the height of the industrial era when we were all supposed to be rational and unemotional. Our challenge is to bring caring relationships out into the open where they belong. We can begin by finding common ground and cultivating it together.

I hope that I have not fooled you into thinking this is an easy challenge. It will take more than stories and models to make it happen. It will take people committed to holding a life and a task in common in the midst of a changing workplace. It will also take leadership and leaders, the subject of the next chapter.

20

The Need for Leadership and Leaders

> We rarely think about how the process of developing leaders
> may be more like parenting than competing, how fostering a
> new culture may be more like gardening than a military
> campaign, or how we might have to learn to dance with our
> competitors as opposed to wage endless war against them.
>
> . . . FRED KOFMAN & PETER SENGE
> *Communities of Commitment:*
> *The Heart of Learning Organizations*

Leadership is a hot topic in the literature about organizations. New books about it spew forth daily from the printing presses and desktops around the world. One might question the need for more to be written about it. However, I think it is important to understand leadership in the context of community at work, because in the final analysis, that's where leadership begins.

Like you, I have read several books on leadership. I even teach a course on leadership theory for a Masters of Leadership program at a local liberal arts college. I will not attempt to cover all that I have learned about this nebulous concept, but I do believe that there is one truth about leadership and leaders that is worth thinking about as we begin to cultivate common ground and release the power of relationships in the workplace. It is this: leadership is a communal concept.

To say that leadership is a communal concept is to put leadership into context. To put this another way, leadership is a dynamic that occurs in the context of relationships. It emerges when a group of people choose to follow an individual for a period of time whom they believe will meet their needs or help them complete a task. As Gary Wills profoundly wrote in his book *Certain Trumpets*, "The leader most needs followers. . . . the leader is the one who mobilizes others toward a goal shared by leader and followers" (Wills 1994, p. 16).

Referring again to the work of Ernest Bormann (1990) with small work groups, it has been shown that when a group is left on its own to deal with the issue of leadership, leaders emerge from a process of interaction between members of a group who are vying for meaningful roles to play within the group. What's more, the process of working out who will be the leader is more a process of residue than the leader appointment process with which we are so familiar in the workplace. In other words, the person who emerges as the leader is the one left with the role of leading the group after the members of the group have gone through the process of trying on and being confirmed in various roles. The details of this process reveal two phases and several archetypical patterns that might be worth a brief review.

In the first phase, the work group goes through a process of eliminating those who are not qualified to lead. People who try for the role of leader but are not accepted or confirmed in the role often drop out in this first phase because they were not able to demonstrate to the satisfaction of the majority of the group that they were qualified to deal with the task or to look out for the best interests of the people. Thus the person who knows little or nothing about the task is often eliminated early in the process as is the one who comes on too strong or appears to be only looking out for himself or herself.

It has been appropriately stated that when the dust settles, the people know who really cares for the task and the people and thus whom to follow.

In phase two of the process of leader emergence, things heat up. Bormann's studies show that usually at least two people emerge from the first phase as contenders for the role of leader. Often these contenders struggle for the role until a strong supporter swings the majority of the group in a direction of support for one over the other. If the contender for leader who was not supported by the group does not find a meaningful role at this point as a task specialist or a healthy devil's advocate, he or she often turns into a central negative figure who seeks to undermine the work of the group. I suspect that we have all experienced the central negative figure on occasion, and if we are honest with ourselves, we would have to admit that we have filled the role once or twice with our own negative attitudes and behaviors.

Several patterns of leader role emergence have been observed in small work groups. In some groups a crisis precipitates a leader who steps forward, in which case the leader must continue to perform or the group will go back to start the struggle all over again. In more productive groups, a leader emerges early on and stays in the role until a new task is taken on. Groups that never resolve the role of leader or in which no one steps forward and mobilizes the group toward a life and a task in common do not seem to do well.

When these studies have been applied to real life in the workplace, where people most often are appointed to the role of leader, they have shown that the process of role emergence either accelerates or becomes caught in a vicious unproductive circle that is stressful for the members of the group. The critical factor that determines the course of the group appears to be whether the person appointed would have been chosen by the followers had the process been allowed to follow its natural course. If the person appointed leader is the same person who would have emerged anyway, the process accelerates and the group becomes productive quickly. When this happens people seem to enjoy their respective roles and each other. If, on the other hand, the appointed leader does not emerge as the natural leader, the group quickly falls into the dysfunctional patterns discussed in chapter 15, such as fighting and running away from conflict or moving into a perpetual pattern of looking for a "real" leader to emerge and make everything all better. In some groups an informal role structure emerges; the appointed leader is placed in a figurehead role while the natural leader mobilizes the group.

Perhaps the most important lesson to be learned from observing work groups in their natural course is that leadership is indeed a communal concept, a consensus between a leader and a group of followers to work together to hold a life and a task in common. When viewed in this way, the role of leader sounds more like a calling than a reward, which is the way we have viewed the role of leader in the organization for years. A promotion to a leadership role was sought by every aspiring young achiever. Little did he or she know that the role of leader is saved for the one who is willing to go the extra mile, to care for the task, and to care for the people.

It is easy to become confused about leadership and the role of leader. If for no other reason, the number of books and articles written about leadership, not to mention the programs designed to develop the "right" leadership skills, can overwhelm us. From all the evidence, one could say that as a culture we are obsessed with leadership. Perhaps because we have such mixed feelings about it. While we aspire to be leaders, we also wish to appear humble and deserving. We much prefer being called upon over forcing our power on others. Our political candidates frequently announce that they will not run for office, only to change their mind the very next day because of "overwhelming support." We also like to believe that we all can share the role of leader at the same time. Yet studies show that groups are far more effective and fun to be in when one person assumes the role of leader for a period of time. Thus shared leadership might more accurately mean rotating the role of leader to match the skills and the willingness of the individual to lead to the task at hand. Leadership is a complicated phenomenon. But there is one thing that all great leaders have in common: followers.

As we move to organizational structures based on teams and virtual communities and hopefully learn how to cultivate common ground in the spirit of caring communities at work, it is important to understand the phenomenon of leadership and followership and the role of leader. Without caring leaders who are willing to step forward, we will not build the relationships needed to hold a life and a task in common. These same caring leaders will know when it is time to step into a new role and let others lead. As the Tao reads, "When the work is done, the goal achieved, the people will say, 'We did it naturally'."

21

The Future Is Ours if We Learn to Care for Each Other

And a youth said, Speak to us of Friendship.
And he answered, saying:
Your friend is your needs answered.
He is your field which you sow with love and reap
    with thanksgiving.

                    . . . KAHLIL GIBRAN   *The Prophet*

The world of work is changing. And people are caught in the middle of the change. On one hand we are told that the old command-control structures of the industrial era will no longer work; on the other, we are given only fragments of the new. We live in what William Bridges, author of *Managing Transitions* and other books on change, called the *neutral zone* (Bridges 1991, 1994). In the neutral zone, old ways no longer work, and new ways are yet undefined. At times, we aren't sure of who we are or where we are going. Perhaps the great poet A. E. Housman captured the feelings of many people of our time when he wrote the famous words: "I, a stranger and afraid, in a world I never made."

There is one thing of which we can be certain in this time of rapid change and uncertainty. People will continue to thrive on meaningful relationships with their work and each other. Oh, we can continue to deny that we need each other, wave a friendly "hello" and go on our merry way as if we live in a world where it is everyone for himself or herself. In truth, one of the main concerns I have about programs to fix our work and our society is that we are making the same mistake we made in the industrial era. I hear a renewed call for individualism. Advice such as "take charge of your own career" can be good advice as long as we do not forget that the self is formed and made stronger in its relationships. I hear consultants tout concepts such as creating "Me, Inc." I have even heard "Soul, Inc." used to describe individual spirituality. But as the great Carl Jung reminded us, "The soul is for the most part outside the body." In other words, the soul is manifested in our relationships with nature, our work, and each other.

At times it appears as if we have traded the instrumental individualism of the industrial era, which is based on the assumption that the rugged individual can make it on his or her own and deserves happiness through success (ironically, gained through loyalty to the organization). We have traded it for the expressive individualism of the information age, which is based on the assumption that the individual must be free to express him- or herself through a well-rounded, balanced life free from loyalty to anyone or any organization. Characters played by John Wayne may have been replaced with those played by Tim Allen on "Home Improvement" and Candice Bergen on "Murphy Brown," but it is still everyone for himself or herself.

Don't get me wrong. This book is not intended to muffle the call for personal responsibility. On the contrary, I believe we need to crawl out from under the shadows of the organization and take control of our work. But we must do it together if we are going to succeed. We must tap into the power of relationships. We must turn over the soil packed by the feet of those who have trampled on our relationships, often for the sake of the organization. We must discover common ground in our shared humanity and learn to cultivate it together without losing our sense of self. We must move from *I* to *we* without losing *me*.

One way to look at the neutral zone is to think of it as a place of opportunity. It's like the good news–bad news game turned around. The bad news is the organization is falling apart; the good news is the organization is falling apart. And it's about time. For years we have been denying caring relationships at work. Worse yet, we have allowed the organization and those who are in power to drive caring relationships underground. It's about time we brought them out into the open where caring relationships belong, where they are free to bring their energy to our work, our work communities, and ourselves as individuals.

How will we bring caring relationships out into the open? It isn't as if some people haven't been trying. Where do we start?

Cultivating common ground while caring for each other will be easier for some than for others. Too many of us learned how to distance ourselves from our work and each other. We learned how to hide behind the invisible shield called "the organization" in order to avoid getting our hands dirty and our hearts wounded. Consequently, we aren't practiced in the art of caring for our work and each other. And because we aren't practiced at it, we are afraid of each other. For some of us, learning to care for our work and each other with our hands, our heads, and our hearts will require embracing our fears and changing our basic assumptions about people and work.

Fortunately, we have help. People are beginning to recognize the need for caring relationships and are doing something about it. As a result, metaphors for building community are emerging even at work. One of the richest metaphors is gardening. As I travel across the country I have noted that people are planting gardens again, not just in their backyards, but in their communities and in open lots in the countryside. In my own community the movement has been popularized and even has an official name: the Community Supported Agricultural Movement. The Internet has hundreds of websites for those who want to share information and advice. It seems that people are rediscovering the joy of working the soil with their hands. They are also rediscovering the joy of working with their hearts. They are releasing the power of caring relationships while cultivating common ground together. The popularity of gardening suggests to me that this rich metaphor could have meaning in the workplace as well as the community.

Where will we plant these gardens? I have given you some ideas already, but I can think of more places where the soil is rich and ready to be turned over. Some of these places are inside the organization itself in small work groups, departments, divisions, and teams. Other places where the soil is rich can be found at the edges of the organization where people join to offer their services for a time. Charles Handy calls them portfolio people because they offer a portfolio of services to the new organization (Handy 1994). Portfolio people also can be gardeners who help organizations build community and discover the joy of caring relationships. There is rich soil to be cultivated around common issues and concerns that cross organizational boundaries where people meet to share, learn, and grow in formal groups or over breakfast once a week. I know of a group of managers who meet weekly to discuss common leadership issues. I also know of a group of executives who meet for one day once a month to talk about ways that business can help solve global issues, such as the population crisis, environmental abuse, and violence. I am sure that you can add examples of your own. The point is, there are plenty of opportunities to cultivate common ground together.

The role of work organizations in the creation of a better world has been widely discussed. Some see large business corporations as playing an important role in establishing global relationships. And no doubt they will. But there is another important role for the organization that is closer to home. In a world where connections to family, community, and church are being redefined, work plays an increasingly important role. Work is where people express themselves, learn how to get along with others, and even find spiritual meaning. Most of the people I interviewed for this book reported that their best friends were from work. Even more interesting, more people experienced what they called a spiritual relationship at work than they did at church. Work is a place where the spirit of community can grow and flourish. Ironically, the organization that we so often criticize for its coldness and inhuman characteristics may contain the seeds for a new work community.

Throughout this book I attempt to show by example, metaphor, a model here and there, and a process how we might begin to build caring communities at work. I use the metaphor of gardening to describe what community at work might look like and how people might relate to each other. But I realize that I cannot build a community at work for you. You must build community on your own with the help of others like you who care. In truth, that is the only way community is built, when a group of people make a conscious commitment to holding a life and a task in common. Examples, metaphors, models and processes help, but real community is built through action. It is a nitty-gritty process of learning to work together and discovering common ground in the process. The good news is, the joy is in the building.

After all is said and done, the process of building community starts with each of us caring for one person, trying to make the world a special place for one human being. With that thought in mind, I close this book with one last story. The story doesn't come from the workplace. It is a story about a little boy and his grandpa. But it is the best example I have of what it means to know someone who truly cares—even when we are human and make mistakes. And isn't that what community is all about?

Epilogue
A Weekend with Grandpa

School was out at last! Out the door and down the gravel road he ran as fast as his little legs could carry him. Over the old wooden bridge and past the little stream he ran. Any other day he might have stomped his feet on the loose boards of the bridge just to hear the echo or meandered down to the riverbank to skip a stone. But there was no time for dallying today. His mind was on one thing and one thing only.

He didn't slow down until Grandpa's place was in full view. He half expected to see Grandpa waiting outside in the yard, but a quick scan of the landscape revealed no one. Slowly, he approached Grandpa's and his favorite hangout: the woodshed. As he moved closer, a voice rang out from inside.

"Is there someone out there? I sure could use some help in here."

Those were the magic words. The little boy ran to the door of the woodshed and grabbed the old leather strap that served as a door handle. He threw his weight against the door, expecting it to fight back as it always did when it scraped the dirt that had accumulated at its base over the years. To his surprise, it opened quickly. A ray of light from the late afternoon sun broke through the open door and never stopped until it landed on the gold buckles of Grandpa's overalls. The little boy could see him now, standing in the far corner reaching for one of several horse harnesses that hung in a neat row on the woodshed wall.

"So there you are. I was beginning to wonder whether I would have to plow the field all by myself." Grandpa finished these words with a look of mischief in his eye as he pulled the harness off the wall and positioned it around his broad shoulders.

For the next half hour the little boy became Grandpa, and Grandpa became Prince, his favorite work horse. They plowed row after row, stopping only after Grandma had called them for supper at least six times.

In the kitchen, the smell of pork chops quickly drew his attention to the table. Next to three succulent chops stood bowls of potatoes, gravy, sweet corn, and a plate stacked with homemade bread—an array of food reserved for the threshing crew or special holidays at home. For a moment he felt sorry for his unfortunate brothers and sisters who were likely fighting back home over a bowl of macaroni and cheese. But the feeling passed quickly when Grandpa plopped a big juicy chop on his plate. He was tempted to pick up the meat and take a big bite right then and there, but he knew that Grandma would insist on a prayer before the meal. He looked up in time to see Grandpa smile and wink at him. They both bowed their heads as Grandma recited grace.

The pork chops were every bit as juicy and delicious as he had anticipated they would be. Even a frown from Grandma didn't stop him from picking up a bone to suck out the last ounce of flavor. Besides, he did it only after watching Grandpa do the very same thing.

Stuffed with food and tired from having plowed all those furrows with Prince, he was content to follow Grandpa into the living room. His tired little body dropped into the soft pillow in the middle of the couch as if it were made just for him. Grandpa sat in his big gray chair and lit up a Chesterfield. Soon a blue curl of smoke drifted to the ceiling. The little boy watched his grandpa purse his lips around the cigarette, then slowly inhale until a hot red coal formed at the tip. It seemed as if the smoke disappeared until finally Grandpa exhaled and a blue cloud rose toward the ceiling. The little boy watched every move his grandpa made with a look of admiration.

He wasn't certain what time he had fallen to sleep. He remembered the beginning of a detective show on TV and assumed that he must have dozed off and been carried to bed by Grandpa. The thought pleased him. But it was morning now and he knew the day would be full of fun and adventure. He peeked over at Grandpa hoping he would see him move. It was only 6:00 and Grandpa normally stayed in bed until at least 6:30, but with a little fidgeting he was able to grab Grandpa's attention.

"I suppose we could get up," Grandpa yawned.

The boy dressed quickly, which wasn't hard to do given the fact that Grandpa had removed only his trousers before putting him to bed the night before. He ran to the kitchen where Grandma was busy frying eggs and bacon. Once again, he thought about his brothers and sisters back home eating the same old cereal and toast. "Lucky me," he thought as Grandpa joined him and Grandma for breakfast. Grandpa cut his egg with a spoon and scooped it onto his toast before taking a bite. The boy, of course, did the same.

After breakfast, the little boy and his grandpa marched off to the woods to pick raspberries, their empty pails swinging to the rhythm of their stride. Soon the pails were overflowing with berries. Grandpa assured him that he was the very best berry-picker who had ever shook a bush. He knew it was possibly a stretch of the truth, but he accepted the praise readily nonetheless.

On the way home they stopped at the corncrib and picked out the best corn silk they could find. Grandpa fashioned two mustaches from the silk, one for each of them. They approached Grandma in the garden with their pails full of berries and their faces plastered with long curly mustaches.

"Who in the world are these strangers?" Grandma asked with a perplexed look that could have fooled anyone into thinking she really didn't know. Grandpa and the little boy looked at each other and winked.

After a quick lunch of sandwiches and fresh raspberries with cream and sugar, Grandpa retired to his big gray chair for a nap. The little boy wandered off to kill some time while waiting for his Grandpa to take him fishing. He wandered into Grandpa's office. There on the desk was an open pack of Chesterfields. He pulled a long cigarette out and pursed it in his lips the way he recalled his grandpa doing it. He stuck out his chin as he mimicked a long exhale and watched the imaginary smoke curl its way to the ceiling. His daydream was interrupted by a sharp voice from the door.

"What's going on in here?" the voiced barked. It was Grandpa and he was mad. "Leave those alone now and go play." Grandpa's words were harsh, and they stung the little boy in a place where his grandpa had never stung him before. He wandered off behind the woodshed.

It seemed like hours before he mustered up the courage to walk back to the house. But the clock on the kitchen wall revealed that only ten minutes had passed. He peaked around the kitchen door to see if Grandpa was still sleeping in his big gray chair. Before he could get a full look, a soft hand touched him on the shoulder and a tender voice announced: "I have been looking all over for you. The worms are dug and ready for fishing. All I need is a partner."

The little boy needed no further coaxing. He looked up at his grandpa with a sheepish smile that was welcomed in return with the warmth of acceptance. Hand in hand they strolled to the creek.

This time the little boy had time not only to look at his reflection and skip a stone across its smooth surface but also to wade in its cool ripples. He even caught a fish or two. All the while Grandpa smiled and reassured him that he was loved and special.

The little boy never forgot his weekend with Grandpa. Later, when he was a grown man assigned to lead others, he would reflect on the pain he felt when his grandpa rebuked him but how wonderfully reassuring it was to be forgiven. He knew what it was like to feel special, especially when one needed reassurance. He strove to watch for those around him who might be feeling the pain of rebuke or rejection because of something he or someone else said or did. He tried to make them feel special again. And every now and then it worked. When it did, he wondered whether his grandpa knew what a wonderful gift he had bestowed on the world with a smile, a wink, a few kind words, the warmth of his presence, and a willingness to forgive.

References

Argyris, Chris. 1993. *Knowledge for Action: A Guide for Overcoming Barriers to Organizational Change*. San Francisco: Jossey-Bass.

Autry, James. 1991. *Love and Profit: The Art of Caring Leadership*. New York: William Morrow.

Axelrod, Robert. 1984. *The Evolution of Cooperation*. New York: Basic Books.

Bales, Robert F. 1950. *Interaction Process Analysis: A Method for the Study of Small Groups*. Reading, MA: Addison-Wesley.

Bales, Robert F. 1970. *Personality and Interpersonal Behavior*. New York: Holt, Rinehart and Winston.

Bateson, Gregory. 1979. *Mind and Nature: A Necessary Unity*. New York: Bantam.

Becker, Ernest. 1973. *The Denial of Death*. New York: The Free Press.

———. 1975. *Escape from Evil*. New York: The Free Press.

Bellah, Robert N., Richard Madsen, William M. Sullivan, Ann Swidler, and Steven M. Tipton. 1985. *Habits of the Heart*. New York: Harper & Row.

———. 1992. *The Good Society*. New York: Vintage.

Bender, Sue. 1989. *Plain and Simple*. New York: HarperCollins.

Bettelheim, Bruno. 1960. *The Informed Heart*. New York: Macmillan.

Bochner, Arthur P., and Clifford W. Kelly. "Interpersonal Competence: Rationale, Philosophy, and Implementation of a Conceptual Framework."*The Speech Teacher* XXIII, no. 4 (November 1974): 279–301.

Bohm, David. 1980. *Wholeness and the Implicate Order*. London: Ark Paperbacks.

Bormann, Ernest. 1990. *Small Group Communication: Theory and Practice*. 3d ed. New York: Harper & Row.

Bridges, William. 1991. *Managing Transitions*. Reading, Mass.: Addison-Wesley.

———. 1994. *Job Shift*. Reading, Mass.: Addison-Wesley.

Buber, Martin. 1958. *I and Thou*. New York: Charles Scribner's Sons.

Buechner, Frederick. 1982. *The Sacred Journey*. New York: HarperCollins.

———. 1991. *Telling Secrets*. San Francisco: HarperCollins.

Byham, William. 1988. *Zap! The Lightening of Empowerment*. New York: Harmony Books.

Collins, James C. and Jerry I. Porras. 1994. *Built to Last*. New York: Harper Business.

Conrad, Charles. 1985. *Strategic Organizational Communication*. New York: Holt, Reinhart and Winston.

Csikszentmihalyi, Mihaly. 1990. *Flow: The Psychology of Optimal Experience*. New York: Harper & Row.

———. 1993. *The Evolving Self*. New York: HarperCollins.

Damasio, Antonio R. 1994. *Descartes' Error: Emotion, Reason, and the Human Brain*. New York: Avon Books.

De Laslzo, Violet Staub. 1959. *The Basic Writings of C. G. Jung*. New York: The Modern Library.

Depree, Max. 1989. *Leadership Is an Art*. New York: Dell Publishing.

Erikson, Erik H. 1980. *Identity and the Life Cycle*. New York: W. W. Norton.

Etzioni, Amitai. 1993. *The Spirit of Community*. New York: Simon & Schuster.

Fox, Matthew. 1994. A New Vision of Livelihood for Our Time. San Francisco: HarperCollins.

Frangos, Stephen J. 1993. *Team Zebra*. Essex Junction, Vt.: Oliver Wight.

Frankl, Viktor. 1984. *Man's Search for Meaning*. Boston: Beacon.

Friedman, Maurice, ed. 1965. *Martin Buber: The Knowledge of Man*. New York: Harper & Row.

Goffman, Erving. 1959. *The Presentation of Self in Everyday Life*. New York: Doubleday.

Hackman, Richard J., ed. 1990. *Groups That Work (and Those That Don't)*. San Francisco: Jossey-Bass.

Hagberg, Janet. 1994. *Real Power*. rev. ed. Salem, Wis.: Sheffield.

Hall, Edward. 1976. *Beyond Culture*. New York: Doubleday.

Handy, Charles. 1994. *The Age of Paradox*. Boston: Harvard Business School Press.

Huizinga, Johann. 1970. *Homo Ludens: A Study of the Play Element in Culture*. New York: Harper & Row.

Jung, Carl. 1959. *The Basic Writings of C. G. Jung*. Ed. V. S. De Laslzo. New York: Random House.

Konner, Melvin. 1987. *The Tangled Wing: Biological Constraints on the Human Spirit*. New York: Harper & Row.

Kotter, John P. 1988. *The Leadership Factor*. New York: Free Press.

Lasch, Christopher. 1984. *The Minimal Self*. New York: W. W. Norton.

Lee, Dorothy. 1987. *Freedom and Culture*. Prospect Heights, Ill.: Waveland Press.

Lipnack, Jessica, and Jeffery Stamps. 1993. *The Teamnet Factor*. Essex Junction, Vt.: Oliver Wight.

Mackay, Harvey. 1990. *Beware the Naked Man Who Offers You His Shirt*. New York: William Morrow.

Mead, George H. 1967. *Mind, Self and Society*. Chicago: The University of Chicago Press.

Miller, Sherod, Daniel Wackman, Elam Nunnally, and Carol Saline. 1982. *Straight Talk*. New York: Signet.

Mumford, Lewis. 1963. *Technics and Civilization*. New York: Harcourt.

Nonaka, Ikujiro, and Hiro Takeuchi. 1996. *The Knowledge-Creating Company: How Japanese Companies Create the Dynamics of Innovation*. Oxford, England: Oxford University Press.

Nouwen, Henri J. M. 1972. *The Wounded Healer*. New York: Doubleday.

Olmsted, Michael S., and Paul A. Hare. 1978. *The Small Group*. New York: Random House.

Palmer, Parker. "Community, Conflict, and Ways of Knowing." *Change* 19, no. 5 (September–October 1987): 20–25.

———. 1983. *To Know as We Are Known*. San Francisco: Harper & Row.

Peck, M. Scott. 1987. *The Different Drum: Community Making and Peace*. New York: Simon & Schuster.

Rifkin, Jeremy. 1995. *The End of Work*. New York: Putnam.

Rogers, Carl R. 1961. *On Becoming a Person*. Boston: Houghton Mifflin.

Schor, Juliet. 1991. *The Overworked American*. New York: HarperCollins.

Senge, Peter. 1994. *The Fifth Discipline*. New York: Doubleday.

Shils, Edward A. 1951. "The Study of the Primary Group." In *The Policy Sciences*. Ed. Daniel Lerner and Harold P. Lasswell. Hoover Institute Series. Stanford, CA: Stanford University Press.

Solomon, Robert. 1990. *Love: Emotion, Myth, and Metaphor*. Buffalo NY: Prometheus Books.

Stack, Jack. 1992. *The Great Game of Business*. New York: Doubleday.

Terry, Robert W. 1993. *Authentic Leadership: Courage in Action*. San Francisco: Jossey-Bass.

Thurow, Lester. 1993. *Head to Head*. New York: Warner Books.

Weick, Karl E. 1979. *The Social Psychology of Organizing*. 2d ed. New York: Random House.

Weisbord, Marvin R. 1992. *Discovering Common Ground*. San Francisco: Berrett-Koehler.

Wheatley, Margaret J. 1994. *Leadership and the New Science*. San Francisco: Berret-Koehler.

Whyte, David. 1994. *The Heart Aroused*. New York: Doubleday.

Wills, Garry. 1994. *Certain Trumpets: The Call of Leaders*. New York: Simon & Schuster.

Wright, Robert. 1994. *The Moral Animal*. New York: Vintage Books.

Index

Argyris, Chris, 74, 114, 117, 118, 155
Asch, Solomon, 122
Assembly effect, 104
Asserting oneself, fear of. *See* Speaking out, fear of
Assumptions about relationships at work, 103-114
    assembly effect as, 103-105
    caring as weakness as, 108-110
    closeness leading to loss of control as, 106-107
    conflicts is about winners and losers as, 110-111, 149
    emotions out and rational decisions as, letting, 107-108
    groups of, basic, 155-156
    losing one's identity as, 105-106
    self protection as, 115-120
    socializing and, no time for, 112-113
Autry, James, 25, 27, 38, 93, 103
Axelrod, Robert, 58

Bales, Robert, 125, 162
Bateson, Gregory, 56, 91
Becker, Ernest, 71, 74, 75, 81
Behavioral flexibility, 154
Bellah, Robert, 12, 18, 68, 97, 108, 119
Bender, Sue, 121, 143
Bennis, Warren, 78
Bettelheim, Bruno, 72, 82, 86, 87, 88
Bion, Wilfred, 155, 156
Blake, Robert, 92
Bochner, Arthur, 153, 154
Bohm, David, 3, 61

Bormann, Ernest. 104, 124, 125, 138, 139, 140, 158, 182, 183
Borysenko, Joan, 85
Bridges, William, 187
Bringing relationships into the open, 53-96
    embracing our fear of each other and, 67-83
    four reasons to care and, 55-65
    from *I* to *we* without losing *me* and, 85-96, 189
Buber, Martin, 36, 91, 105
Buechner, Frederick, 13, 86
Building capabilities diagram, 179
Building relationships, 135-142
Building strong selves, 11
Byham, William, 59

Caring
    claims of, 7
    contagious factor of, 59-60, 177
    goodness of, 56-57, 58-59
    implications of, 6
    meaning of, 6-7
    power of, 57, 60-63
    reasons for, four, 55-65
    responding to, 6-7
    responsibility of, 7
    spirit of, 6
    weakness and, 108-110
Caring and the organizational imperative for growth, 9-11
Caring relationships
    example story of, 48-52
    fun of, 57

Caring relationships, *continued*
  hunger for, 7-9
  managers and, 8
  strong selves made by, 11-13
  teamwork example of, 28-31
  what they are, 4
  where did they go, 5-6
  where to find them, 7
Carter, Forrest, 55
Celebrations, 167-169
Central negative figure, 140
Changing workplace, 177-180
Claims, fear of, 75-76
Claims made by caring, 7
Clock, invention of the, 17
Closeness leading to loss of control,
  106-107
Cohen, Susan, 104
Collins, James C., 27
Common ground, discovering,
  121-128
  creative process diagrams and,
  126, 127
  cultivating and, 189, 190
  effective dialogue conditions
  for, 122
  example of nonworking teamwork
  and, 122-123
  group fantasies and, 125, 126
  how to, 127, 128
  leaders setting stages for, 124
  reason for joining groups and, 124
  symbolic convergence and, 125
Communitarianism movement, 79
Community at work
  building, 171
  example of, 28-31
  leadership and, 181-185
Community, definition of, 28
Competitive nature, 71
Complications of relationships at
  work, 4
Conflict and winners and losers,
  110-111, 149
Conflict, consequences of, 159
Conflict, fear of. *See* Fighting, fear of
Conflict, growing through, 147-159

  approaches for, 153-159
  assumption groups for, 155
  embarrassment and, 155
  example story of, 149-153
  looking at, 149
  parts of life and, 147-148
  peace and, 158
  process approach to, 157-159
  psychoanalytic approach to,
  155-156
  relationships as part of, 148-149
  skills approach to, 153-154
  systems approach to, 154-155
  truths about, 148
Conrad, Charles, 27, 94
Contagious factor of caring, 57, 59-60
Creative process diagrams, 126, 127,
  133, 141, 145, 157, 164
Creativity blossoming, 144
Csikszentmihalyi, Mihaly, 9, 12, 58,
  63, 71, 80, 85, 88, 89, 118, 119,
  130, 131, 132, 144, 161
Cultivating common ground, 97-159,
  189, 190
Cultivation, definition of, 119

Damasio, Antonio, 69, 107, 108
Decisions and emotions, 107-108
Deming, W. Edwards, 10, 40
Denying a drive, 5
Dependency groups, 155, 156
Depree, Max, 25, 27
Descriptiveness, 153
Dialogue, healthy, 73, 74
Differentiation, definition of, 89
Disagreement consequences, 73
Disappointment, fear of, 76-79
Diversity in the workplace, 27
Driving relationships underground,
  1-52
  consequence of, 64
  Hawthorne Revelation and, 23-31
  how we got disconnected and,
  15-22
  new organization and, 33-52
  struggle with relationships at work
  and, 3-13

Drucker, Peter, 37
Dumb-upness, 50

Einstein, Albert, 90
Eisenstat, Russell, 144
Eliot, George, 135
Emerson, Ralph Waldo, 23
Emotions and rational decisions,
    107-108
Empathetic communication, 153
Empowerment, 34, 57
Energy of caring. *See* Power of caring
Enjoyment of caring, 63-64
Entitlement, 20
    end of age of, 38
Environmental stimulation and
    conflict, 158
Erikson, Erik, 148
Ethic of progress, driving forces
    behind, 19
Etzioni, Amitai, 28, 79
Evolutionary psychology and caring,
    58, 60
    being cautious and, 70
Expressive individualism, 12
Extension transference, 87

Fear of each other, embracing, 67-83
    claims and responsibilities and,
        75-76
    disappointment and, 76-79
    fighting and, 72-74
    loss of self and, 80-82
    relationships and, 69
    responsibilities and claims and,
        75-76
    speaking out and, 74-75
    unknown and, 70-72
Fight-or-flight groups, 155, 156
Fighting, fear of, 72-74
Fiutak, Thomas, 158
Fox, Matthew, 38, 133
Frangos, Stephen, 25, 59
Frankl, Viktor, 88, 129, 130, 131,
    133
Freedom, definition of, 88
Friedman, Maurice, 105

Fun in caring, 57, 63-64
Future if we learn to care, 187-191

Gemeinschaft (community), 19
Generalized other, 81
Generativity, definition of, 119
Gesellschaft (society), 19
Getting along at work, best way for, 4
Gibran, Kahlil, 187
Goffman, Erving, 62, 73, 80, 111, 117
Golden handcuffs, 16
Good for us, caring is, 56-57, 58-59
Group dynamics, 127
Group fantasies, 125, 126
Groups, reason for joining, 124
Growing through conflict, 147-159
Growth, caring, and the organiz-
    ational imperative for, 9-11

Hackman, Richard, 104-105, 123, 124
Hagberg, Janet, 109
Hall, Edward T., 15, 20, 57, 87, 106,
    112, 144
Halo effect, 24, 25
Handy, Charles, 38, 79, 107, 171, 190
Hare, Paul, 25, 26
Harmony, 89, 90, 105
    conflict and tension and, 162, 163
    definition of, 88, 162
    living in, 161-166
    meaning and, 131
    societies with, learning from, 91-92
Harvard Business School. *See*
    Hawthorne Revelation
Harvey, Paul, 18
Hawthorne effect, 24
Hawthorne Revelation (studies),
    23-31, 57, 179
    conducted by, study, 23
    lessons to be learned from, 26
    revelation in, 55
Healthy relationships, importance
    of, 39
Hillel, 1
Houseman, A. E., 36, 187
How we got disconnected, 15-22
Huizinga, Johann, 57, 63, 64

Human behavior and goodness of
  caring, 58
Human relationship issue, 38
Human relationship seminars, 38
Humility, false, 75
Hunger for caring relationships, 7-9

Identity, losing one's, 105-106
Implications of caring, 6
Individualism, 188
Industrial era, 5, 9, 10, 21, 83, 179
  commandment-control structures
    of, 187
  community connections and, 18
  defining work and, 16
  game of business and, 63
  heroes of, 68, 109
  individualism and, 188
  managerial-therapeutic thinking
    of, 20
  mistakes by, 12
  organizational structures of, 107
  responsibility avoidance and, 76
  self and, 80
  unrealistic pictures of, 77
Inequities of opportunity, 86
Informal minisocieties, 26
Informal relationships, definition
    of, 6
Informal structure, 139
Instrumental individualism, 12

Johnson, President Lyndon, 149
Jung, Carl, 21, 39, 67, 81, 82, 91, 188

Keller, Helen, 135
Kelly, Clifford, 153, 154
Kofman, Fred, 181
Konner, Melvin, 55, 58
Kotter, John, 37
Kushner, Rabbi, v

Lasch, Christopher, 12
Leaders setting stages for working
    together, 124
Leadership and leaders, need for,
    181-185

commonality of, 184
communal concept of, 182, 184
contestant elimination and,
    182-183
importance of, 183
Leadership, obsession with, 184
Lee, Dorothy, 88, 89, 90, 91, 105, 106
Lindbergh, Anne Morrow, 92, 94, 161
Lipnack, Jessica, 177, 178
Living in harmony, 161-166
Locke, John, 18
Losers and winners and conflict,
    110-111
Losing face, fear of, 74
Loss of self, fear of, 80-82
Loyalty, death of, 38
Luria, A. R., 144

Mackay, Harvey, 71, 117
Madsen, Richard, 97
Mandela, Nelson, 75
Mead, George Herbert, 61, 81
Meaning
  creative process diagram and, 133
  definition of, 130
  discovering, 130, 131-132, 133
  harmony and, 131
  relationships and, 133
  resolve and, 131
Miller, Sherod, 72
Moore, Thomas, 167
Mossman, James Frank, 42, 169
Mumford, Lewis, 16, 17

Natural drives transference, 87-88
Neglected relationships, price paid
    for, 40
Neutral zone, 187, 189
New organization, the, 33-52
Nonaka, Ikujiro, 104
Nouwen, Henri, 109
Nurturing relationships and sowing
    seeds, 135-142
  example of, 137-138
  role emergence processes and, 139,
    140, 183
  role taking and, 139

roles to vie for and, 139
work group hurdles and, 138

Olmsted, Michael, 25, 26
Organization versus self, 19
Organization's energy, 20
Organizational man, 80
Organizational structures, 178, 179
Owning feelings and thoughts, 154

Pairing groups, 155, 156
Palmer, Parker, 6, 28, 38, 147, 169
Parable for this book, xi-xv
Peck, M. Scott, 156, 157, 158
Porras, Jerry I., 27
Portfolio people, 190
Positive energy of caring,
      understanding, 61
Power of caring, 57, 60-63
Power of relationships, releasing, 41
Primary tension, 162, 163
Process approach to growing
      through conflict, 157-159
Process for building community at
      work, 97-159
   clearing out old assumptions and,
      103-114
   discovering common ground and,
      121-128
   fertilized with meaning and,
      129-133
   from swords to plowshares and,
      115-120
   growing through conflict and,
      147-159
   metaphor and, what's in a, 99-101
   nurturing relationships and
      sowing seeds and, 135-142
   sowing seeds and nurturing
      relationships and, 135-142
   starting to, 191
   working the soil together and,
      143-146
Psychoanalytic approach to growing
      through conflict, 155-156
Pyramidal hierarchy, 17

Rational decisions and emotions,
      107-108
Reason(s) to care, 55-65
   contagious factor as, 57, 59-60
   fun factor as, 57, 63-64
   goodness factor as, 56-57, 58-59
   power factor as, 57, 60-63
Reciprocal altruism, 58
Redfield, Robert, 19
Relationships
   building, 56, 91
   conflict and, 148-149
   fear of, 69
   importance of, 62
   nurturing, 135-142
   option of, 56
   respect and, 91
   romantic type of, 78
Relationships and the new organiz-
      ation, 37, 171-191
Relationships at work
   assumptions and, clearing out old,
      103-114
   example of, 92-93
   meaning and, 133
   metaphor for, 99-101
   spiritual type of, 191
   unnaturalness of, 94
Responsibilities, fear of, 75-76
Responsibility of caring, 7
Rifkin, Jeremy, 86
Rights granted to organizations by
      us, 10
Risks by caring, 3-4
Rituals, 167-169
Rogers, Carl, 87
Role distancing, 117, 118
Role emergence processes, 139, 140,
      181-185
Role taking, 139
Roles to vie for, 139
Romantic relationships, reason for,
      78
Rousseau, Jean Jacques, 19

Secondary tension, 162, 163

Self
 defining, 78
 development of, 81, 91
 fear of loss of, 80-82
 shaping of, 21
 sharing, 91
Self disclosure, 154
Self protection assumptions, 115-120
Self versus organization, 19
Self versus society, 19
Self worth, 62
Self-esteem and fighting, 73
Seminars on human relationships, 38
Senge, Peter, 28, 114, 181
Sense of self, harming, 36
Settlement, definition of, 119
Shils, Edward, 26
Skills approach to growing through
 conflict, 153-154
Smith, Adam, 18
Socializing at work, no time for,
 112-113
Solomon, Robert, 68, 69, 77, 78
Speaking out, fear of, 74-75
Spirit of caring, 6
Spiritual relationships at work, 191
Stack, John, 57
Stamps, Jeffrey, 177, 178
Strong selves are made from caring
 relationships, 11-13
Struggle with relationships at work,
 3-13
 caring and the organizational
 imperative for growth and, 9-11
 hunger for caring relationships
 and, 7-9
 strong selves are made from caring
 relationships and, 11-13
 time to care and, 13
 what does it mean to care and, 6-7
 where did caring relationships go
 and, 5-6
Suffering as meaning, 130
Sullivan, William M., 97
Sunday neurosis, 88
Swidler, Ann, 97
Symbolic convergence, 125, 158

Systems approach to growing
 through conflict, 154-155

Takeuchi, Hirotaka, 59-60, 104
Taylor, Frederick, 20
Team that doesn't work example,
 122-123
Team Zebra. See Frangos, Stephen
Teamnets, 178
Teams at work, overdoing, 11
Teams for teams' sake, 35
Tensions, 162, 163
Terry, Robert, 158
Thurow, Lester, 37
Time for caring, 13
Tipton, Steven M., 97
Tonnies, Ferdinand, 19
Transitional times, 40-41

Unknown, fear of, 70-72

Virtual community, 140, 141, 178,
 179, 184
 example of, 42-47
 meaning of, 47

Weakness and caring, 108-110
Weick, Karl, 154
Weisbord, Marvin, 114, 121, 122, 124,
 165
Western Electric Company. *See*
 Hawthorne Revelation
Wheatley, Margaret, 53, 107, 114, 177
Whyte, David, 38
Wills, Gary, 182
Winners and losers and conflict,
 110-111
Work group hurdles, 138
Worker productivity study,
 improving. *See* Hawthorne
 Revelation
Working together, 143-146
 common ground and, 146, 189, 190
 creative process diagram and, 145
 creativity and, 144
Workplace, the changing, 177-180
Wright, Robert, 58, 59

Butterworth-Heinemann Business Books ... for Transforming Business

5th Generation Management: Co-creating Through Virtual Enterprising, Dynamic Teaming, and Knowledge Networking, Revised Edition
Charles M. Savage, 0-7506-9701-6

After Atlantis: Working, Managing, and Leading in Turbulent Times
Ned Hamson, 0-7506-9884-5

The Alchemy of Fear in the Workplace
Kay Gilley, 0-7506-9909-4

Beyond Strategic Vision: Effective Corporate Action with Hoshin Planning
Michael Cowley and Ellen Domb, 0-7506-9843-8

Beyond Time Management: Business with Purpose
Robert A. Wright, 0-7506-9799-7

The Breakdown of Hierarchy: Communicating in the Evolving Workplace
Eugene Marlow and Patricia O'Connor Wilson, 0-7056-9746-6

Business and the Feminine Principle: The Untapped Resource
Carol R. Frenier, 0-7506-9829-2

Choosing the Future: The Power of Strategic Thinking
Stuart Wells, 0-7506-9876-4

Cultivating Common Ground: Releasing the Power of Relationships at Work
Daniel S. Hanson, 0-7506-9832-2

Flight of the Phoenix: Soaring to Success in the 21st Century
John Whiteside and Sandra Egli, 0-7506-9798-9

Getting a Grip on Tomorrow: Your Guide to Survival and Success in the Changed World of Work
Mike Johnson, 0-7506-9758-X

Innovation Strategy for the Knowledge Economy: The Ken Awakening
Debra M. Amidon, 0-7506-9841-1

The Intelligence Advantage: Organizing for Complexity
Michael D. McMaster, 0-7506-9792-X

Intuitive Imagery: A Resource at Work
John B. Pehrson and Susan E. Mehrtens, 0-7506-9805-5

The Knowledge Evolution: Expanding Organizational Intelligence
Verna Allee, 0-7506-9842-X

Leadership in a Challenging World: A Sacred Journey
Barbara Shipka, 0-7506-9750-4

Leading from the Heart: Choosing Courage over Fear in the Workplace
Kay Gilley, 0-7506-9835-7

Learning to Read the Signs: Reclaiming Pragmatism in Business
F. Byron Nahser, 0-7506-9901-9

Leveraging People and Profit: The Hard Work of Soft Management,
Bernard A. Nagle and Perry Pascarella, 0-7506-9961-2

Marketing Plans That Work: Targeting Growth and Profitability
Malcolm H.B. McDonald and Warren J. Keegan, 0-7506-9828-4

A Place to Shine: Emerging from the Shadows at Work
Daniel S. Hanson, 0-7506-9738-5

Power Partnering: A Strategy for Business Excellence in the 21st Century
Sean Gadman, 0-7506-9809-8

Putting Emotional Intelligence to Work: Successful Leadership is More Than IQ
David Ryback, 0-7506-9956-6

Resources for the Knowledge-Based Economy Series

The Knowledge Economy
Dale Neef, 0-7506-9936-1
Knowledge Management and Organizational Design
Paul S. Myers, 0-7506-9749-0
Knowledge Management Tool
Rudy L. Ruggles, III, 0-7506-9849-7
Knowledge in Organization
Laurence Prusak, 0-7506-9718-0
The Strategic Management of Intellectual Capital
David A. Klein, 0-7506-9850-0

*Setting the PACE® in Product Development: A Guide to Product and
Cycle-time Excellence*
Michael E. McGrath, 0-7506-9789-X

Time to Take Control: The Impact of Change on Corporate Computer Systems
   Tony Johnson, 0-7506-9863-2

The Transformation of Management
   Mike Davidson, 0-7506-9814-4

What is the Emperor Wearing? Truth-Telling in Business Relationships
   Laurie Weiss, 0-7506-9872-1

Who We Could Be at Work, Revised Edition
   Margaret A. Lulic, 0-7506-9739-3

Working From Your Core: Personal and Corporate Wisdom in a World of Change
   Sharon Seivert, 0-7506-9931-0

To purchase any Butterworth-Heinemann title, please visit your local bookstore or call 1-800-366-2665.

Related Butterworth-Heinemann Titles

The Breakdown of Hierarchy
Communicating in the Evolving Workplace
Eugene Marlow ◆ Patricia O'Connor Wilson

1997   176pp   0-7506-9746-6   pb $17.95

Leadership in a Challenging World:
A Sacred Journey
Barbara Shipka

1996   240pp   0-7506-9750-4   pb $17.95

A Place to Shine:
Emerging from the Shadows at Work
Dan Hanson

1996   208pp   0-7506-9738-5   pb $17.95

Learning to Read the Signs:
Reclaiming Pragmatism in Business
Steve Heath

1997   192pp   0-7506-9901-9   pb $17.95

Feel free to visit our web site at: http://www.bh.com

These books are available from all good bookstores or in case of difficulty call:
1-800-366-2665 in the U.S. or +44-1865-310366 in Europe.

E-Mail Mailing List
An e-mail mailing list giving information on latest releases, special promotions/ offers and other news relating to Butterworth-Heinemann business titles is available. To subscribe, send an e-mail message to majordomo@world.std.com. Include in message body (not in subject line) subscribe bh-business